McDonald's® Glassware

Joyce and Terry Losonsky

Schiffer Publishing Ltd

4880 Lower Valley Road, Atglen, PA 19310 USA

Library of Congress Catalog Card Number: 99-62569

Designed by Bonnie M. Hensley
Type set in Zapf Humanist Dm BT/Humanist 521 BT

ISBN: 0-7643-0879-3
Printed in China
1 2 3 4 a

Published by Schiffer Publishing Ltd.
4880 Lower Valley Road
Atglen, PA 19310
Phone: (610) 593-1777; Fax: (610) 593-2002
E-mail: Schifferbk@aol.com
Please visit our web site catalog at
www.schifferbooks.com

In Europe, Schiffer books are distributed by
Bushwood Books
6 Marksbury Avenue Kew Gardens
Surrey TW9 4JF England
Phone: 44 (0)181 392-8585;
Fax: 44 (0)181 392-9876
E-mail: Bushwd@aol.com

This book may be purchased from the publisher.
Include $3.95 for shipping. Please try your bookstore first.
We are interested in hearing from authors with book ideas on related subjects.
You may write for a free printed catalog.

Acknowledgments

The authors would like to express our sincere appreciation and gratitude to all our collector friends who have contributed their time and knowledge to our research. In the event of oversight, we sincerely apologize for any names and familiar faces left off our ever-growing list of friends met on the collecting trail.

Gerald & Helen Buchholz
Mark Carder
John & Brenda Clark
Ken Clee
Ron & Eileen Corbett
John & Darlene Drew
Mike & Deanna Fountaine
Jimmy & Pat Futch
Fred & Doris Heubner
Sharon Jarrett
Brian Jones
John & Eleanor Larsen
Willy Monfils
Bill & Pat Poe
Lari & Manuella Poli
Neal Reinert
Varinda Rojanaumphai
Natalie & Jean Claude Royer
Rich & Laurel Seidelman
Pat Sentell
Bill Thomas
David Tuttle
Lloyd & Nancy Washburn
Frank & Janet Zamarippa

Contents

Introduction

Welcome to the world of McDonald's glassware! Starting from meager offerings in the early sixties to an abundance of promotions in the eighties and nineties, McDonald's has creatively advertised their products through the sale of collectible drinking glasses. Spearheading regional promotions with regional advertising, McDonald's continuously focuses on the growing number of consuming patrons who enjoy collecting advertising memorabilia.

During our country's bicentennial year of 1976, McDonald's led the parade of fast food glasses with the McDonaldland Action Series and Collector Series. The Libbey and Brockway Glass Companies' styling provided wonderful glasses to collect!

In the eighties, the success of the two earlier series was followed by the McDonaldland Adventure series of glasses, plus several series of sports glasses issued on a regional basis, the Great Muppet Caper glasses, and the over-distributed Camp Snoopy series. The Olympic Mugs Series was then widely distributed, along with regional and national Garfield glasses and mugs. The McVote series asked consumers to vote for their favorite character by purchasing the appropriate glass and casting their ballot. The Big Mac won, hands down! By offering interspersed regional promotions, McDonald's was able to catch the attention of the public in competitive markets—giving McDonald's the advantage. It was not long before national as well as regional attractions were featured on the glassware. Famous American events—local golf championships, for example—as well as sports teams and sports players were illustrated on different size glassware throughout the eighties and nineties. The "hook" was: buy something like a Value Meal and get a free or relatively inexpensive glass to keep the experience fresh in your mind.

In the nineties, McDonald's started to coordinate its advertising with movie releases. This new decade began to unfold with the Nutcracker Series, issued on a regional basis, followed by national issues. The "Together, We've Got What it Takes" slogan in 1992 meant McDonald's was teaming up with major movie productions and advertising for glassware was beginning to take hold. Batman Forever mugs led the nineties' parade of mugs, in conjunction with the release of Batman movies. Several of the promotions in the nineties did not merit glassware; less expensive plastic cups and mugs were the venue of choice instead. Nevertheless, "Great Expectations" was still the theme of the early nineties. Disney cartoon characters and Warner Brothers characters were extremely popular choices for glasses and mugs because of the success of films from these studios, such as *Fantasia, Snow White, Sleeping Beauty, Batman Forever, A Bug's Life, and Lion King II.*

By the mid-nineties, a reality check had set in. The fast food market was not expanding as it had in the seventies and eighties. Fierce competition in the nineties meant business was earned by the competition *losing* business. McDonald's "Glassware To Go®" philosophy dictated a return to regional issues like the Baltimore Orioles glasses, the NASCAR 50th Anniversary glasses, and the Mark McGwire St. Louis set. The competition was keener in certain markets, requiring regional glassware promotions to attract the consuming public away from other fast food choices. A return to basics at McDonald's ushered in the last years of the nineties decade.

The bridge to the twenty-first century—or the moon, for that matter!—will undoubtedly be lit by the Golden Arches spans. In the first decade of the new century, however, the parade of McDonald's glassware will be judged by Y2K kids selectively choosing their magic

Speedee, the McDonald's company symbol used through the early 1960s.

moment to purchase. These knowledgable kids will be daily influenced by advertising from a multitude of electronic media. They will be followed closely by their parents, road weary from so many choices yet still susceptible to mass advertising concerning the latest and greatest collectible glasses not to be missed. These are the parents, after all, who jumped on the Beanie Baby bandwagon and flocked to McDonald's Teenie Beanie Baby promotions. A "Price is Right" philosophy prevails with these parents; that is, the price must reflect the value of the glassware in order for future promotions to be successful.

Bringing up the "tail end" of the consumer parade crossing the bridge to the twenty-first century will be the seniors, an age group garnering more disposable income than their predecessors. Seniors want QSVC (quality, service, value, and cleanliness) plus nostalgia along with their food selections—in line with today's low fat, diet-conscience mindset. Seniors may have given up on their children (or vice versa), but their grandchildren are another story! If a grandchild wants an item, seniors will go to great lengths to secure it. McDonald's is just about the right distance to travel to put smiles on the grandkids' faces. The future looks golden bright for a continuation of collectible McDonald's glassware in the twenty-first century. Ultimately, the journey and the process of collecting become as integral to the experience as the actual acquisition of the glassware itself.

1990s era McDonald's.

1960s era McDonald's.

The Great Muppet Caper glasses, 1981.

McDonald's Salutes Disneyland glasses, 1989.

Translite for NASCAR glasses, 1998.

Helpful Information for Using This Book

Pricing

Note: mint price range (MINT only) listed for all items.

As with most collectible glasses, condition is a paramount factor in determining price. Next to having no chips, brightness of color is probably the second most important factor for glasses. Close to color brightness is clear lettering and logo markings—missing letters or marks detract considerably from the item's price. Glasses which have seen the inside of a dishwasher are basically not collectible. Additionally, oversubscribed glasses command little price. The regional availability of a particular series of glasses, the limited sponsorship of a series, or the scarcity of a particular issue also influence price, although the electronic media is currently changing this perception. Electronic auctions such as eBay are leveling the playing, i.e., the buying/selling, field. Price variations between items available on the west coast and those on the east coast are becoming insignificant. Advances in electronic mail and auction availability are also exerting a considerable influence on price fluctuations. Before long, one price will be reflective of an item's value and not the wide ranges listed for some glasses and mugs. In some cases, a person's access to the electronic media or no access to the media will make a significant difference in the price paid. In the end, price is determined between the buyer and the seller. This book is intended as a useful guide to decision-making concerning the availability and price of McDonald's glassware.

$—— indicates no definitive price has been established

Glass Condition

Mint - NO chips. NO scratches. NO fading. NO dishwasher spots. NO registration problems.

Good - Glass can have noticeable bubble or slight imperfections. NO chips. NO scratches. NO fading. Slight registration problems.

Poor - Small chip in rim or crack in glass.

Glass Terms

BM - Bottom of glass

Brockway - describes a type of thick, heavy glass that tapers from top to bottom (1970s style)

Federal - describes a type of straight sided glass

Flare - describes a type of Coca-Cola glass which has big flare at the top of the glass

Heavy - describes a glass that has 1/4" to 1/2" thick glass at the base

Indented - describes the base of a glass which decreases towards the bottom

Pedestal - describes the base of a glass which looks like a pedestal

Numbering System

The numbering system for each item in this book includes a Gl for glass or mug, followed by the year of distribution, followed by a numerical listing of the items. The authors' intention is to reflect a different alphabetical/numerical listing for each glassware item distributed.

Example: Gl8210 = McDonald's Arches Tankard

Gl = Glass or mug
82 = Year of distribution
10 = Numerical listing of item

About This Book

The goal of this book is to illustrate and describe a wide variety of McDonald's glassware, including mugs and steins from the United States as well as international glassware. The world of plastic cups given out by McDonald's is too vast to include in this text and will be covered in future books. Our selections are not intended as a comprehensive, all-inclusive listing of the glassware distributed at the stores and/or at Owner/Operator meetings. Rather, the items shown are representative of the types and kinds of glassware collectors may encounter—wherever they travel and whatever auction they may participate in.

We do not pretend to be authorities on the intricacies of glasses and glassware companies. We do, however, hope this listing will expand our readers' knowledge of the vast assortment of glassware given out by McDonald's during the last thirty-six years and provide a format for readers to organize their own collections. In order to provide as much information as possible, we have sometimes made reference to known glasses which are not pictured.

In the search for collectible adventure, *McDonald's® Glassware* is intended to be a train car, if not the engine, on the McDonaldland® TO GO Express. Happy collecting!

The Sixties

- **1963 - Speedee as company symbol being phased out**

- **1963 - Bisected Arches as company symbol being phased in**

- **1965 - 1st National Owners Operators Convention**

  Date: October 19-21, 1965
  Place: Hollywood, Florida (Hollywood Beach Hotel)
  Theme: "The Sky's The Limit"

- **1967 - 2nd National Owners Operators Convention**

  Date: October 18-20, 1967
  Place: Miami, Florida (Doral Country Club)
  Theme: "McDonald's is Our Kind of Place"

- **1968 - 1,000th Store Opening in Des Plaines, Illinois**

- **1968 - Regional Meetings:**

  Eastern region:
  Dixville Notch, New Hampshire (Balsam's - 9/17-18)

  Mideast region:
  White Sulphur Springs, West Virginia (Greenbriar CC - 10/14-16)

  Southern region:
  Atlanta, Georgia (Regency Hyatt House - 9/27-28)

  Midwest region:
  Lake Geneva, Wisconsin (Playboy Club - 10/3-4)

  Western region:
  San Diego, California (Bahia Motor Hotel - 10/29-30)

  Theme: "The Customer is #1...What have you done lately for the Customer?"

- **1969 - 3rd National Owners Operators Convention**

  Date: October 20-23, 1969
  Place: Miami, Florida (Doral Country Club)
  Theme: "The Challenge of Success"

Generic Glasses and Mugs, 1960s

❑ **GI6301 Mug - BOSS with Bisected Arches.** Operators and managers of McDonald's stores were encouraged to purchase the BOSS mug so there would be no doubt about who's the boss! Some mugs may be found with the name of the city's mayor, bank president, fire chief, police chief, newspaper editor, or boss name added under the word "BOSS." All mugs will have the bisected arches on one side. Mugs were advertised in the McDonald's newsletter dated October 1963, by the Perlman Paper Company, item No. 125 for $1.85 each. $———

GI6301

❑ **GI6901 Wine Glass - 1,000th Store Opening.** Clear short balloon style wine glass with, "1969 National Operators Convention" and McDonald's bisected arches logo etched. 6" high x 3" diameter on top. $650.00-750.00

The Seventies

1970

- **1,500th Store Opening in Concord, New Hampshire**

Generic Glasses and Mugs, 1970

❑ **GI7001 Character Glass - Ronald.** Balloon style on hollow base. Appears to be smoky, iridescent with a clear bottom. Character is molded into head of hollow glass. Name of each character is molded into the back side of glass. 5 5/8" high x 3 1/4" diameter on top and 2 1/4" base. This set of glasses (GI7001-4) is definitely not up to McDonald's specifications and could be a prototype glass set. $——

GI7001

❑ **GI7002 Character Glass - Big Mac.** Balloon style on hollow base. Appears to be smoky, iridescent with a clear bottom. Character is molded into head of hollow glass. Name of each character is molded into the back side of glass. 5 5/8" high x 3 1/4" diameter on top and 2 1/4 " base. $——

GI7002

❑ **GI7003 Character Glass - Grimace.** Balloon style on hollow base. Appears to be smoky, iridescent with a clear bottom. Character is molded into head of hollow glass. Name of each character is molded into the back side of glass. 5 5/8" high x 3 1/4" diameter on top and 2 1/4" base. $——

❑ **GI7004 Character Glass - Captain Crook.** Balloon style on hollow base. Appears to be smoky, iridescent with a clear bottom. Character is molded into head of hollow glass. Name of each character is molded into the back side of glass. 5 5/8" high x 3 1/4" diameter on top and 2 1/4" base. $——

❑ **GI7005 Wine Glass - 1,500th Store Opening.** Clear short balloon style wine glass (same as 1000th wine glass with "1500th McDonald's" in GOLD color and McDonald's arches logo etched. 6" high x 3" diameter on top. $350.00-500.00

1971

- **4th National Owners Operators Convention**

Date: October 17-21, 1971
Place: Waikiki Beach, Hawaii (Sheraton Waikiki)
Theme: "Success and Then Some"

1972

- **2,000th Store Opening in Des Plaines, Illinois**

- **Regional Meetings:**

East/Mid Atlantic region:
Lancaster, Pennsylvania (Host Farm - 10/15-18)

Mideast region:
Hot Springs, Virginia (Homestead - 10/29 through 11/1)

Southern region:
Miami, Florida (Doral Country Club - 10/11-13)

Midwest region:
Palm Beach, Florida (Breakers - 10/23-26)

Western region:
Monterey, California (Del Monte - 10/1-3)

Theme: "Let's Face It"

Generic Glasses and Mugs, 1972

❑ **GI7201 Wine Glass - 2,000th Store Opening.** Clear short balloon style wine glass (same as 1000th wine glass with "2,000th McDonald's" in GOLD color and McDonald's arches logo etched. 6" high x 3" diameter on top. $____

Left: Plastic cup from 2000th store opening. Right: GI7201

Disposable cup from 4th National Owner Operator Convention, 1972.

1973

- **2,500th Store Opening in Hickory Hills, Illinois**

McDonaldland Character Glass Set (5 5/8" with indented base), 1973

Character Glasses:

❑ **GI7301 Ronald standing with two arms raised**. Red stripes, clear glass. $____

❑ **GI7302 Captain Crook standing with sword**. Red stripes, clear glass. $____

❑ **GI7303 Mayor McCheese standing with finger raised**. Orange stripes, clear glass. $____

❑ **GI7304 Big Mac standing with left foot raised**. Blue stripes, clear glass. $____

❑ **GI7305 Gobblins standing.** Red stripes, clear glass. $____

❑ **GI7306 Grimace standing, drinking shake**. Yellow stripes, clear glass with "Evil" Grimace imprinted. $____

GI7301-03

GI7304-06

GI7305

GI7306

Comments: The McDonaldland Character Glass Set of 1973 appears to be the first planned "set" of McDonald's glasses illustrating the McDonaldland characters. The concept of "planned" means that it was advertised in the 1973 Rogers Merchandising Gift Catalogue. The set was obviously produced prior to April 1973. It is listed in McDonald's Gift Catalog as "NEW FOR '73" on page 13. The listing states: "Everyone's favorite McDonaldland characters—on glasses. Set of six glasses features Ronald McDonald, Hamburglar, Big Mac, Captain Crook, Gobblin and the Evil Grimace." The Evil Grimace name is on one glass, but NOT Evil Grimace's picture with four arms; Grimace with only two arms is depicted on the glass. Additional catalog information reads: "Bright McDonaldland colors. 1-4 @ $6.65 set, 5-9 @ $5.90 set, 10-20 @ $5.75 set." The picture accompanying the description illustrates Mayor McCheese instead of Hamburglar as listed and two Gobblins instead of one Gobblin. It is plausible that the set of six glasses was only produced in very limited quantities, perhaps as preproduction samples, due to copyright decisions being made by McDonald's at that time period. The character representations on the glasses were not up to McDonald's standards. Specifications were clearly redesigned for all the characters in 1973 by McDonald's Specification Manual. Anything regarding character representation that was outside the specifications—as these glasses clearly were—was cancelled. Furthermore, the character of Grimace was undergoing a major change in early 1973, from "Evil Grimace" to just "Grimace." Evil Grimace, shown with four arms, appeared on items given out during the 1971-1972 time period only. Trademarks were registered in 1973 depicting Grimace without the three hairs on his head, as illustrated on the Evil Grimace glass. Different color stripes appear at the top and bottom of the "white" band around the glasses. Glass is a clear glass with indented base. For further details and discussion, see listings for GRIMACE and EVIL GRIMACE in our book, *McDonald's Pre-Happy Meal Toys from the Fifties, Sixties and Seventies.*

Plastic cup from 1973 2500th store opening (on right)

Generic Glasses and Mugs, 1973

❑ **GI7307 Wine Glass 2,500th Store Opening.** Long stemmed clear wine glass, imprinted in gold lettering, gold logo, "2,500th," 7" high x 2 1/2" top diameter. Store Opening distributed a plastic cup marked with "2,500th" and date. Wine glass, each
$25.00-40.00

❑ **GI7308 Ceramic Stein.** White ceramic stein, slightly flared out towards the bottom with McDonald's logo in black and yellow. Advertised in ParaGifts Catalogue 1973-77 and K Promotions Gift Catalogue 1977.
$25.00-35.00

GI7308

Monogrammed Glasses, 1973

❑ **GI7309 Monogrammed Glass Tankard.** Etched monogram glass tankard flanked by the arches on each side of the monogrammed initials. 17 ounce.
$25.00-35.00

❑ **GI7310 Monogrammed Glass Tumbler.** Etched monogram glass flanked by the arches on each side of the monogrammed initials. 13 ounce. $25.00-35.00

❑ **GI7311 Monogrammed Highball Glass.** Etched monogram glass flanked by the arches on each side of the monogrammed initials. 9 ounce. $25.00-35.00

❑ **GI7312 Monogrammed Old Fashion Glass.** Etched monogram glass flanked by the arches on each side of the monogrammed initials. 5 1/2 ounce.
$25.00-35.00

Comments: Few known examples of these glasses exist outside of the prototypes shown. This set is listed in the 1973 and later catalogue listings.

GI7309-12

1974

- **3,000th Store Opening in Woolwich, England** - England's first McDonald's

- **Regional Meetings:**

East/Mideast & New York:
San Francisco, California (St. Francis - 3/7-10)

Mid Atlantic & Los Angeles region:
Dallas, Texas (Fairmont - 2/28-3/1)

Midwest region:
San Francisco, California (St. Francis - 3/4-7)

San Francisco region:
San Francisco, California (St. Francis - 2/25-28)

Boston region:
Marcos Island, Florida (3/17-20)

Atlanta & Dallas region:
Marcos Island, Florida (3/21-24)

Theme: "Nothing Recedes Like Success"

- **International Congress Meeting**

Place: London, England (New London Center)
Date: November 13-14, 1974

Generic Glasses and Mugs, 1974

❑ **GI7407 Wine glass 3,000th Store Opening.** Long stemmed tapered wine glass, with United States' flag and Great Britain's flag in red, white, and blue on front. "3,000th" printed in blue under UK flag; "London '74" in blue on side of US flag. 8 1/2" high x 2 1/8" diameter at top. Glass may be viewed at the Ray Kroc Museum in Chicago.
$25.00-40.00

❑ **GI7408 Pedestal Coffee Cup.** White milk glass pedestal coffee mug/cup with gold arches and black McDonald's logo. Numbered Mc 0077 in catalogue.
$7.00-10.00

GI7408

Headline Glasses and Mugs, 1974

Headliner Glasses:

❑ **GI7409 All-American Team Winner**
$20.00-35.00

❑ **GI7410 Crewman of the Year**
$20.00-35.00

❑ **GI7411 Crewwoman of the Year**
$20.00-35.00

❑ **GI7412 Crewman of the Month**
$20.00-35.00

❑ **GI7413 Crewwoman of the Month**
$20.00-35.00

❑ **GI7414 Opens First Store**
$20.00-35.00

❑ **GI7415 Opens Another Store**
$20.00-35.00

❑ **GI7416 Graduates From H.U.**
$20.00-35.00

Comments: Headline glasses/mugs came as clear glass with black and white newspaper overlay. Newspaper headlines on the sides of each glass were from nine selections plus personalized name leading to the headlines. One name and headline per set of eight glasses. Sold by the set or sold four mugs per set. Set of eight glasses was listed in the 1974 ParaGifts catalogue as Number MC 0235 and sold for $11.50 per set; set of four mugs was listed as MC 0236 and sold for $10.85.

1975

• 20th Anniversary McDonald's

Place: Palmer House & Civic Center, Chicago, Illinois
Date: April 15-16, 1975

Glasses To Go (short 5", heavy, NOT marked with words, "Collector..."), 1975

Character Glasses:

❑ **GI7501 Big Mac standing with one hand holding police whistle.** $8.00-10.00

❑ **GI7502 Captain Crook standing with sword/point side down.** $10.00-14.00

GI7501-06

- ❑ **GI7503 Grimace standing with arms outstretched, white mouth.** $18.00-24.00
- ❑ **GI7504 Hamburglar holding open cape with both arms.** $10.00-14.00
- ❑ **GI7505 Mayor McCheese standing and holding eyeglasses with one hand.** $8.00-10.00
- ❑ **GI7506 Ronald sitting with legs crossed.** Black outline on costume, black lettering for name, "Ronald McDonald," NO SERIES NAME on glass. $10.00-14.00

From left: GI7606, Collector Series II; GI7512, Collector Series I (regular version, no black outline on Ronald); GI7506.

Comments: Glasses To Go, 5" Brockway style, were made by Brockway Glass Company. They were 5" short, heavy glasses with straight sides, deep color and NOT IDENTIFIED as Collector Series. Glasses had character graphics with name of character underneath. The words "Collector Series" DO NOT APPEAR on the glass. This was a test promotion run in the Boston region.

The Collector Series I (5 5/8" / LIGHTER color with "Collector.." on glass), 1975

Note: two different size "Collector Series" glasses exist: 5 5/8" and 5 3/4"; they are called Collector Series I and II regardless of size.

Character Glasses:

- ❑ **GI7507 Big Mac standing.** Black lettering. $7.00-10.00
- ❑ **GI7508 Captain Crook standing with sword.** Black lettering. $10.00-14.00
- ❑ **GI7509 Grimace standing.** Light purple color, red mouth, blue lettering. $18.00-24.00

Left: GI7603, Collector Series II; Right: GI7509, Collector Series I (lighter color Grimace glass).

- ❑ **GI7510 Hamburglar with cape.** Black lettering. $10.00-14.00
- ❑ **GI7511 Mayor McCheese standing.** Black lettering. $7.00-10.00
- ❑ **GI7512 Ronald sitting with legs crossed.** Red/yellow color, red outline, lettering in red, fingers closed stance. $10.00-15.00
- ❑ **GI7513 Ronald Variation: Ronald sitting with legs crossed.** Black outline, lettering in black, fingers closed stance. $20.00-35.00

Comments: Collector Series I is an indented bottom glass, 5 5/8", with "Collector Series" on the glass in different colors: four glasses from this series have the lettering under the glasses in BLACK, while glasses with Ronald have RED LETTERING and those with Grimace have BLUE LETTERING. Four of these glasses were repeated in the Collector Series II set due to popular demand for the series; on the fifth and six glasses (Ronald and Grimace), the color of the lettering was changed to black (see page 21). Series I had a variation of Ronald, which consists of Ronald in black outline with his hands in closed finger stance. Two different size "Collector Series" glasses exist—5 5/8" and 5 3/4"—which is probably due to production variation. This series includes variations of character portrayal on the glasses. Grimace in Series I has a red mouth, white eyes, and lettering in blue. Series I has Ronald without the black outline, lettering in red. As noted, a variation of Ronald exists where the black outline was added to the closed finger stance. Additionally, after changing from all red and yellow to red, yellow, and black, the designers apparently decided to also change Ronald's hands to show open fingers. This latter appearance shows up in Collector Series II (1976).

Generic Glasses and Mugs, 1975

❑ **GI7514 Wine Glass: 20th Anniversary.** Balloon style wine glass with "Congratulations from Lily" in black on back and 20th logo in gold and black on front.
$20.00-35.00

GI7514

❑ **GI7515 Multi-language Glass: Big Mac "Special sauce..." saying.** Straight sided glass with indented base. Six bands of text in yellow, red, black, black, yellow, and red surround the glass. Top band is "Big Mac" in five different languages separated by arches logo. The other five bands have "Two all beef patties special sauce lettuce cheese pickles onions on a sesame seed bun" in English, German, Italian, Spanish, and Greek.
$7.00-10.00

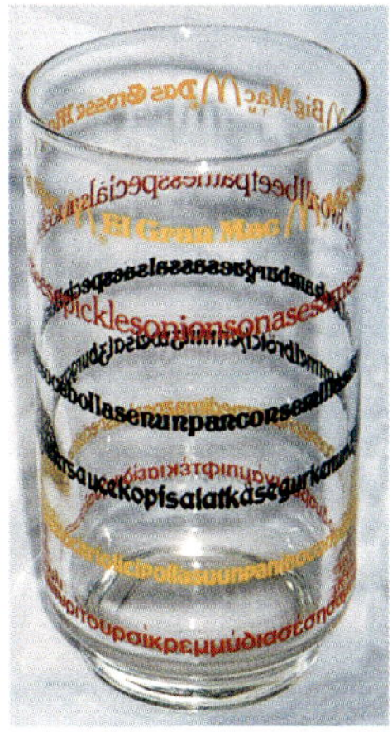

GI7515

❑ **GI7516 H.U. 10,000 Student Glass.** Pedestal glass depicting Hamburger University building, "Class #209 November 6, 1975" in black. Outer green band with gold lettering and HU logos. Marked Hamburger U I.
$15.00-25.00

❑ **GI7517 Coffee Mug - Employee.** White pedestal mug with red/gold logo. Employee's name is imprinted in red. 5 1/4" high x 2 3/4" diameter at top with 3 3/8" diameter at base.
$15.00-25.00

❑ **GI7518 Ceramic Stein - 20th Anniversary.** White ceramic stein mug with Ray Kroc and historic McDonald's events graphics. 4" high x 3 1/2" top. Ceramic mug was given out at party in Chicago, April, 1975.
$25.00-45.00

GI7518

❑ **GI7519 Ceramic Stein - 1975 Orlando.** Cream ceramic stein mug with logo in gold and blue, "You, You're the One" in blue on front and "How Ya Managing? Orlando, Florida 1975" in blue on back. 3 3/4" high x 2 7/8" diameter at top. $15.00-25.00

1976

- **4,000th Store Opening in Montreal, Canada**

- **Regional Owner/Operators Meetings:**

Boston Zone:
Orlando, Florida (Orlando Hyatt - April 25-28)

Chicago Zone:
Kauai, Hawaii (Kauai Surf - May 2-5)

Columbus Zone:
Kauai, Hawaii (Kauai Surf - May 7-10)

LA Zone:
Kauai, Hawaii (Hawaii Surf - May 10-13)

Canada Zone:
Kauai, Hawaii (Hawaii Surf - May 14- 17)

Theme: "The Challenging World of Number One"

The Collector Series II (5 5/8", black lettering, "Collect All 6 Glasses To Go"), 1976

Collector Series protoype glasses

Assortment of McDonald's glasses, including Collector Series.

Character Glasses:

- ❑ **GI7601 Big Mac standing.** Black lettering. $8.00-10.00
- ❑ **GI7602 Hamburglar with cape.** Black lettering. $10.00-14.00
- ❑ **GI7603 Grimace standing.** WHITE mouth with black lettering. $18.00-24.00
- ❑ **GI7604 Mayor McCheese standing.** Black lettering. $8.00-10.00
- ❑ **GI7605 Captain Crook standing with sword.** Black lettering. $10.00-14.00
- ❑ **GI7606 Ronald sitting with legs crossed.** Black lettering, fingers open stance. $10.00-14.00

GI7601-03

GI7604-06

From left: GI7506, GI7513, GI7512, GI7606

From left: GI7603, GI7509, GI7503

Comments: The Collector Series II glasses were very similar to the 1975 series of Glasses to Go except that this promotion was a national one. Series II had all the characters outlined in black with black lettering. All have the words "Collector Series" on the glass. The same graphics were featured but the glasses were 1/2" taller (5 5/8" made by Libbey Glass Company instead of 5" glasses made by Brockway). Names of the characters appeared underneath the character picture with the words "Collector Series" on the glass. Glasses have indented bases.

The Ronald glass in Series I (1975) was initially made with red and yellow paint colors (NO BLACK). It appears this portrayal of Ronald did not show off Ronald's best feature: his hands. Thus, the color black was added on the next run and Ronald's hands were changed to show open fingers. Additionally, Grimace in Series I was shown with feet apart, looking flat footed. This was also changed in the next run, when black was added. The black made Grimace's mouth disappear, so white was added to replace the

red. The final set of glasses, therefore, would have all black lettering.

Pre-production samples, prototype glasses exist. Changes were made to the uniformity of lettering colors, the black outline was added, and Ronald's fingers were changed to an open stance. NOTE: the Hamburglar glass shown in the photo on page 21 is faded; it has obviously been run through the dishwasher a number of times and has little value with collectors. Prices quoted are for mint glasses, not faded glasses.

McDonaldland Action Series Glasses, 1976, 1977, 1983

Four different sizes of the McDonaldland Action Series glasses are known to exist.

The Short Short Series I (4 7/8" - 5") 1976 was test marketed in St. Louis, Missouri during 1976. It was a regional promotion in 1976.

McDonaldland Action Series glasses in three sizes. Left to right: 6 1/8", 5 5/8", 4 7/8"

The Short Series II (5 5/8") 1977 with indented base was nationally distributed during the summer of 1977. Controversy arose over the lead content of the ink used on the glasses. In July 1977, McDonald's suspended distribution of this set due to the suspected lead. A federal Task Force investigated the safety of the decorated glasses and found McDonald's glasses posed no hazard to public health in normal use. In many stores, only the Ronald glass had been distributed. The stores voluntarily recalled the glasses involved. These glasses were made by Libbey Glass and had an indented base. They were later test marketed in St. Louis during May-June 1978 and introduced regionally in the USA from August through December 1978, or while the supply lasted. Listed under 1977.

The Tall Series III (6 1/8") 1977 was made by Anchor Hocking. These glasses had white line art graphics, the character name under the graphic, and "1977 McDonaldland Action Series" under the name. Listed under 1977.

The Embossed Arches Series IV (5 5/8") 1983. This fourth series of McDonaldland Action Series glasses has embossed "M" arches circling the bottom of the glass as well as molded into the bottom of the glass. They were apparently distributed in Southern California on a very limited basis—samples have been found primarily at Southern California flea markets. Since research indicates they probably originated in Southeast Asia or Japan, it is likely they were designed for the international market and only sporadically distributed in the USA. Listed under 1983.

McDonaldland Action Short Short Series I (4 7/8" - 5"), 1976

Character Glasses:

❑ **GI7607 Big Mac on roller skates.** $15.00-20.00

- ❑ **GI7608 Captain Crook on a boat.** $15.00-20.00
- ❑ **GI7609 Grimace with pogo stick.** $15.00-20.00
- ❑ **GI7610 Hamburglar on flat car.** $15.00-20.00
- ❑ **GI7611 Mayor McCheese with camera.** $15.00-20.00
- ❑ **GI7612 Ronald playing leapfrog.** $15.00-20.00

Comments: Regional promotion, test marketed in St. Louis, Missouri during 1976 and reissued in 1982 with the 1982 date. Size variation is due to production mold differences. 4 7/8" high.

Generic Glasses and Mugs, 1976

- ❑ **GI7613 Water Goblet Regional Owners Operators Meeting.** Water goblet glass with circular brown logo of a fish with date, "1976 McDonald's Owner/Operator Convention" on glass in brown lettering. 4 1/4" high x 2 7/8" diameter at top. $10.00-15.00

- ❑ **GI7614 Wine Glass 4,000th Store.** Balloon pedestal clear wine glass with red lettering. One side had phrase in English, second side had phrase in French, "To commemorate the Opening of the 4,000th McDonald's Store September 9th Montreal, Canada. McDonald's Canada" in red. 5 1/2" high x 3 1/8" diameter at top. $25.00-35.00

- ❑ **GI7615 Pedestal Mug - All American Team.** All American Team logo on front of 11 oz. porcelain pedestal mug. $15.00-20.00

- ❑ **GI7616 Stein - All American Team.** White porcelain 16 oz. stein holds liquid or pencils. All American logo on front with McDonald's logo in gold and black on reverse side. $25.00-35.00

GI7616

- ❑ **GI7617 Good Morning, America! Mug.** White milk glass mug with arches and sun. 3 1/2" high x 3/4" indented base. Says "Good Morning" in orange with "TM" by logo. This was the first breakfast mug promotion. The same mug ran in Canada, with the addition of the Canadian Leaf logo. Handle was rectangle shaped as opposed to the later issued round shape handle. $.50-1.00

GI7617

GI7617

GI7617

❑ **GI7618 Breakfast Brigade Mug.** White milk glass mug with "breakfast brigade" and arches with sun. Handle was rectangle shaped as opposed to later issued round shape handle. $.50-1.00

❑ **GI7619 Breakfast Brigade Mug.** White milk glass mug with "breakfast brigade" and arches, NO SUN. $.50-1.00

❑ **GI7620 Coffee Mug - Security Analysts.** White ceramic coffee mug with red and yellow logo, "Security Analysts Conference October 20 & 21, 1976" in black on front. On the reverse side is a Net Income Graph 1966-76 in black and green. 4" high x 3 1/2" diameter at top. $10.00-20.00

Sports Mugs / Smoked Glass Mugs, 1976

Character Smoked Glass Mugs:

❑ **GI7621 Captain Crook hitting a baseball.** $5.00-7.00

❑ **GI7622 Grimace shooting a basket.** $5.00-7.00

❑ **GI7623 Hamburglar as hockey goalie.** $5.00-7.00

❑ **GI7624 Ronald throwing a football.** $5.00-7.00

Comments: Mugs were regionally distributed in the Southwest and Hawaii during the summer of 1976. Smoked glass mugs have embossed designs appearing twice around the mugs with the character names beneath the character' s feet. McDonald's arch logo is on the bottom of the mug.

GI7621-24

GI7621-24

1977

- **Happy Meal concept is tested**

McDonaldland Action Short Series II (5 5/8"), 1977

Character Glasses:

- ❑ **GI7701 Big Mac on roller skates.** $4.00-7.00
- ❑ **GI7702 Captain Crook on a boat.** $4.00-7.00
- ❑ **GI7703 Grimace with pogo stick.** $4.00-7.00

GI7701-03

- ❑ **GI7704 Hamburglar on flat car.** $4.00-7.00
- ❑ **GI7705 Mayor McCheese with a camera.** $4.00-7.00
- ❑ **GI7706 Ronald playing leapfrog.** $4.00-7.00

GI7704-06

Comments: The McDonaldland Action Short Series II (5 5/8") with indented base was nationally distributed during the summer of 1977. Controversy arose over the lead content of the ink used on the glasses. In July 1977, McDonald's suspended distribution of this set due to the suspected lead. A federal Task Force investigated the safety of the decorated glasses and found McDonald's glasses posed no hazard to public health in normal use. In many stores, only the Ronald glass had been distributed. The stores voluntarily recalled the glasses involved. These glasses were made by Libbey Glass and had an indented base. They were later test marketed in St. Louis during May-June 1978 and introduced regionally in the USA from August through December 1978, or while the supply lasted.

McDonaldland Action Tall Series III (6 1/ 8"), 1977

Character Glasses:

❑ **GI7707 Big Mac on roller skates.** $8.00-10.00

❑ **GI7708 Captain Crook on a boat.** $8.00-10.00

❑ **GI7709 Grimace with a pogo stick.** $8.00-10.00

❑ **GI7710 Hamburglar on a flat car.** $8.00-10.00

❑ **GI7711 Mayor McCheese with a camera.** $8.00-10.00

❑ **GI7712 Ronald playing leapfrog / BRIGHT yellow and BRIGHT red.** $8.00-10.00

GI7707-12

Comments: The Tall Series III (6 1/8") 1977 was made by Anchor Hocking. These glasses had white line art graphics with each character's name under the graphic and "1977 McDonaldland Action Series" under name.

Generic Glasses and Mugs, 1977

❑ **GI7713 Dinner Dance RMH.** Ronald McDonald House Dinner Dance, October 15, 1977 drink glass. $40.00-75.00

GI7713

❑ **GI7714 Family Picnic Mustache Mug.** White ceramic "mustache mug" with green and yellow graphics. Features characterization of man and woman in a canoe on front. "8th Annual Old Fashioned Family Picnic, Nestlerest Park, Lake Zurich, IL Sunday July 10, 1977" on back. Mint in white cardboard box came with two paper black mustaches. Mint in box. $75.00-100.00

GI7714 (front)

GI7714 (back)

❑ **GI7715 Store Managers Stein.** Heavy glass stein marked "1977 Store Manager' s Convention" in red letters with red and gold logo. Stein features a gold colored cowboy on horse graphic. 5 1/2" high x 1 7/8" diameter at base. $25.00-40.00

❑ **GI7716 San Diego Stein.** Heavy glass stein marked, "1977 Store Manager's Convention July 10-12 San Diego" in red lettering with red and yellow logo. 5 1/2" high x 1 7/8" diameter at base. $25.00-40.00

❑ **GI7717 Washington D.C. Stein.** Heavy glass stein marked, "1977 Store Manager' s Convention July 27-29 Washington D.C." in red lettering with red and yellow logo. 5 1/2" high x 1 7/8" diameter at base. $25.00-40.00

1978

• **5th National Owners Operators Convention**

Place: Las Vegas, Nevada (Las Vegas Hilton)
Theme: "When We Work At It—It Works"

• **5,000th Store Opening in Fujizawa City, Japan**

Commemorative program from 5000th store opening.

Pittsburgh Steelers / Super Bowl XIII Sports Glasses, 1978

❑ **GI7801 Davis.** $5.00-7.00
❑ **GI7802 Shell.** $5.00-7.00
❑ **GI7803 Stallworth.** $5.00-7.00
❑ **GI7804 Webster.** $5.00-7.00

Comments: Four glasses comprised the series celebration. The name for each glass comes from the first player to the right of the arches on each glass. Glasses were sold for $.79 each in regional area.

GI7801-03

GI7801-04

Seattle Seahawks Sports Glasses, 1978

- ❑ **GI7805 Beeson, Ellen, Beamon.** $8.00-10.00
- ❑ **GI7806 Boyd, Gregory, Tuiasosopo.** $8.00-10.00
- ❑ **GI7807 Raible, McCullum, Zorn.** $8.00-10.00
- ❑ **GI7808 Smith, Largent, Sims.** $8.00-10.00

Comments: Four sports glasses comprised the series. Name comes from right of the arches on each glass. Glasses were sold for $.79 each in regional area. Glasses have indented foot and a pair of blue and green bands encircling the base with Indian Eagle heads facing each other. Each glass has photos of three players with McDonald's logo on the left and "Seattle Seahawks" on the right along with the NFL logo.

GI7805-08

Generic Glasses and Mugs, 1978

❑ **GI7809 Las Vegas Wine Glass.** McDonald's logo and "Las Vegas 1978" on front of wine glass with rim outlined in silver. 7" high x 2 1/2" diameter at top. Originated from Owner/Operators (O/O) Convention in Las Vegas, 1978. $25.00-40.00

❑ **GI7810 Albany Region, New York Wine Glass.** McDonald's logo and "Albany Region 1978" on front of wine glass with rim outlined in silver. 8 1/2" high x 3" diameter at top. $25.00-40.00

GI7810

❑ **GI7811 Albany Region, New York Stein.** McDonald's logo and "Albany Region {within Pirate's Head graphic} Bounty Hunters 1978 Managers Convention" in red lettering. 5 1/2" high. $30.00-50.00

❑ **GI7812 Leadership Conference 1978 Stein.** Cream colored ceramic stein with "Profiles in Leadership 1978" and McDonald's logo in black graphics. Attendee's name is imprinted on back of stein in black. "Buntingware" is imprinted on the bottom of the stein. 6 1/8" high x 3 1/8" diameter at top with 3 3/4" diameter at base. $40.00-50.00

GI7812, shown behind 1979 stein (GI7905)

- ❑ **G17813 Decanter.** Hand blown Lenox crystal "Mariner" Decanter. 42 oz. clear glass. $50.00-75.00

- ❑ **G17814 Tankard.** Handblown Lenox crystal tankard. 16 oz. clear glass. $50.00-75.00

- ❑ **G17815 Juice Glass.** McDonald's logo juice glass with indented base has frosted band around center. 3 5/8" high. $4.00-6.00

- ❑ **G17816 Pedestal Mug.** Breakfast milk glass coffee or milk mug comes with three color band of yellow, orange, and rust. Distributed after the 1976 successful coffee mug of like design. 10 oz. 5 1/2" tall. $7.00-10.00

- ❑ **G17817 Earthen Tankard.** Cream colored ceramic tankard came with black, rust, and yellow stripe under the Golden Arches logo on front. $15.00-20.00

G17813

G17816

G17817

G17815

❑ **GI7818 Sundae Glass.** Clear glass with raised arches around top rim. $5.00-8.00

❑ **GI7819 Beverage Logo Glass.** Clear "Old Fashioned" beverage glass with 3/4" arches etched on the front. 9 oz. glass. $7.00-10.00

❑ **GI7820 Beverage Logo Glass.** Clear "Beverage" glass with 3/4" arches etched on the front. 13 oz. glass. $7.00-10.00

❑ **GI7821 Beverage Logo Glass.** Clear "On the Rocks" beverage glass with 3/4" arches etched on the front. 5 1/2 oz. glass. $7.00-10.00

GI7818

1978 *Chicago Tribune* advertisement for sundae glass in comics.

GI7819-21

1979

- **Sports Glasses issued**
- **Happy Meal concept begins**

Pittsburgh Steelers / Super Bowl XIV Sports Glasses, 1979

❑ **GI7901 Bleier.** $5.00-6.00
❑ **GI7902 Colb.** $5.00-6.00
❑ **GI7903 Davis.** $5.00-6.00
❑ **GI7904 Thornton.** $5.00-6.00

Comments: Set of four clear glasses are 6" tall with yellow, white, and black graphics. Two white parallel lines encircle a line of Golden Arches on the bottom of the glass with the pictures and names of three players on each glass. Glasses sold for $.79 each during the regional promotion.

GI7901-04

Generic Glasses and Mugs, 1979

❑ **GI7905 Profiles in Leadership Stein.** Gray ceramic stein with "Profiles in Leadership 1979" in black lettering with a red line encircling the rim. Stein was given away at the regional Management meeting. 4 5/8" high x 3 1/8" diameter at the top. $25.00-35.00

GI7905

❑ **GI7906 Lead Crystal Glass.** Etched McDonald's arches on the front of glass. Leaded bottoms. 7 oz. $7.00-10.00

❑ **GI7907 Lead Crystal Tankard.** Etched McDonald's arches on front of rounded base glass. $7.00-10.00

GI7906

GI7907

❑ **GI7908 Mike Quinlin 20 Years Mug.** Black ceramic beer mug had a gold rim with McDonald's Golden Arches within a box. "Q" for Quinlin was within the box and "20 Years" beneath box. 5 1/8" high x 3 3/4" diameter at base. $40.00-50.00

❑ **GI7909 Law '79 Mug.** Black ceramic mug with gold rim and golden color Ronald characterization holding Scales of Justice. Marked "Law '79" in gold on front of mug. 4 1/4" high x 2 1/4" x 3 1/8" diameter at base. $40.00-50.00

❑ **GI7910 Oklahoma Glass Stein.** Oklahoma Market Assistant Managers Convention held in Tulsa, Oklahoma in 1979. Came with McDonald's logo graphics in red. 5 1/8" high x 2 3/4" at base. $20.00-35.00

❑ **GI7911 Albany Glass Stein.** Albany, New York Region with pirate's graphics marked "Albany Region Bounty Hunter 1979 Managers Convention" in black. 5 1/8" high x 2 3/4" diameter at base. $20.00-35.00

❑ **GI7912 New York Glass Stein.** Marked "New York Region Managers Convention 1979" in red with New York Street Fighters logo in red and yellow. 5 1/8" high x 2 3/4" diameter at base. $20.00-35.00

❑ **GI7913 Houston Glass Stein.** Marked "Store Managers Convention Houston, Texas July 22-24, 1979" in yellow on red background. McDonald's logo is on front with hands shaking graphics in red and yellow on the back. 6 1/2" high x 3 1/4" diameter at base. $20.00-35.00

❑ **GI7914 Denver Ceramic Mug.** Marked "It's People 1979 Denver, Colorado October 28-30" with McDonald's logo in red. 3 1/2" high x 3 1/4" diameter at top. $7.00-10.00

❑ **GI7915 It's People Ceramic Stein.** Marked "It's People 1979" in red on yellow background graphics. 5 1/8" high x 2 3/4" diameter at top. $7.00-10.00

GI7915

❑ **GI7916 Silver Tankard.** Silver-plated tankard mounted on solid walnut base. Presented for 15 years service to McDonald's. $25.00-50.00

❑ **GI7917 Crystal Pitcher.** Etched lead crystal clear pitcher with McDonald's logo etched in the side. 64 oz. $40.00-75.00

GI7917

❑ **GI7918 International Picnic Stein.** Root beer style stein with "Old Fashioned Picnic McDonald's International 1979" imprinted in red on front of stein. 5 1/8" high x 2 3/4" diameter at top with a 2 1/4" diameter at base. Stein was made by Anchor Hocking. $20.00-35.00

❑ **GI7919 Logo Mug.** Series of ceramic logo mugs made in brown, blue, yellow, or white. McDonald's logo in gold with "TM" in gold also. Mugs came with brown plastic lids. Each $5.00-8.00

GI7919

❑ **GI7920 McDonald's Christmas Mug.** Clear glass mug with red script, "McDonald's Christmas 1979." $10.00-15.00

❑ **GI7921 International Canadian Stein.** "Nobody Can Do It Like McDonald's Can" jingle is imprinted on the front of the stein with McDonald's Canada logo. $20.00-35.00

Left: GI7920; Right: GI8114.

GI7921

The Eighties

1980

- **25th Anniversary of McDonald's**

- **6th National Owners Operators Convention / 25th Anniversary of McDonald's**

  Place: Toronto, Ontario Canada
  Theme: "Our World...Today, Yesterday and Tomorrow"

- **6,000th Store Opening in Munich, Germany**

McDonaldland Adventure Series (6 1/4"), 1980

Character Glasses:

❑ **GI8001 Big Mac nets the Hamburglar.** $7.00-10.00

❑ **GI8002 Captain Crook sails the bounding main.** $7.00-10.00

❑ **GI8003 Hamburglar hooks the hamburgers.** $7.00-10.00

❑ **GI8004 Grimace climbs a mountain.** $10.00-15.00

❑ **GI8005 Mayor McCheese rides a runaway train.** $7.00-10.00

❑ **GI8006 Ronald saves the falling stars.** $7.00-10.00

GI8001-03

Comments: Regional distribution: Northeastern USA. The name of the glass is imprinted above the character graphic on each glass; below the characterization is "McDonaldland Adventure Series." The back of the glass reads "© 1980 McDonald's Corporation." Glasses are drawn with dark line art drawings as graphics with color added. 6 1/4" high.

GI8004-06

Atlanta Falcons Sports Glasses (5 5/8"), 1980

❑ **GI8007 Andrews, Note, Kenn.** $5.00-7.00

❑ **GI8008 Bartkowski, Jackson, Jenkins.** $5.00-7.00

❑ **GI8009 Kuykendall, Curry, Williams.** $5.00-7.00

❑ **GI8010 Thielmann, Butler, Cain.** $5.00-7.00

Comments: Regional distribution in the Atlanta, Georgia area. Names of the players are imprinted along with the team name. 5 5/8" high.

GI8007-10

Philadelphia Eagles Sports Glasses (6"), 1980

- ❑ **GI8011 Bunting.** $5.00-7.00
- ❑ **GI8012 Carmichael.** $5.00-7.00
- ❑ **GI8013 Franklin.** $5.00-7.00
- ❑ **GI8014 Jaworski.** $5.00-7.00
- ❑ **GI8015 Montgomery.** $5.00-7.00

Comments: Set of five glasses comprised the 1980 Philadelphia Eagles set. Glasses have green and white graphics with two player pictures and names per glass. McDonald's logo appeared in black on the glasses. 6" high.

GI8011-14

GI8016

GI8019

Generic Glasses and Mugs, 1980

- ❑ **GI8016 25th Anniversary Mug.** Cream colored ceramic mug with silver attached medallion imprinted with "25th Anniversary April 15, 1980." Mug was given out at the Owners/Operators Convention in Toronto, Canada. 5 5/8" high x 3 1/4" diameter at top and 4 1/4" diameter at base. $25.00-40.00

- ❑ **GI8017 25th Anniversary Brandy Snifter.** Snifter was imprinted "25th Anniversary Toronto, Canada 1980" in silver with a silver rim. Given out at the Owner/Operators Convention in Toronto, Canada. 5 1/2" high x 3" diameter at top and bottom. $25.00-35.00

- ❑ **GI8018 6,000th Store Champagne Glass.** Champagne glass with the McDonald's arches and "6,000th" etched on the front. $25.00-40.00

- ❑ **GI8019 6,000th Store Beer Stein.** Gray ceramic beer stein with McDonald's logo imprinted in blue with "Store 6,000th München, November 1980." $45.00-75.00

❑ **GI8020 6,000th Wine Glass.** Tall, clear wine glass with "Pousse Cafe" in yellow lettering. $25.00-35.00

❑ **GI8021 Daring, First and Different Glass Boot.** Glass boot shaped like a beer stein inscribed with "Be Daring, First and Different" in brown and cream. Given out at the Combined Owners/Operators of Texas Meeting. 6" high. $25.00-40.00

❑ **GI8022 Daring, First and Different Glass Stein.** Stein inscribed with McDonald's logo and "Be Daring First & Different" in blue and white. Given out at the Combined Owners/Operators of Texas Meeting. 5 1/2" h. $25.00-40.00

❑ **GI8023 Daring First & Different Coffee Mug.** White ceramic coffee mug inscribed with "Daring First and Different" in blue. Given out at Combined Owner/Operators Meeting of Texas. 3 1/2" high x 3 1/4" wide. $7.00-10.00

GI8023

❑ **GI8024 Cowboy Boot Glass Stein.** Glass Stein with raised, molded design in red and black. Design shows Santa wearing a western hat inscribed with "Merry Christmas 1980" and McDonald's logo in black. Comes with a glass lid. $35.00-45.00

❑ **GI8025 The Denim Collection Glass.** Glass imprinted in blue and white with denim apparel look. Graphics show tool and dye leather belt with Coca-Cola logo. Glass has "The Denim Collection from McDonald's" encircling the bottom. $5.00-8.00

GI8025

❑ **GI8026 Together Champagne Glass.** Inscribed champagne glass with "Together, McDonald's and You!" in red. $10.00-20.00

❑ **GI8027 Lake Geneva Pedestal Coffee Mug.** Lake Geneva pedestal, milk glass coffee mug inscribed "Lake Geneva Wisconsin 1980" in red. $7.00-10.00

❑ **GI8028 1980 Leadership Conference Mug.** 1980 Leadership Conference cream colored, ceramic mug inscribed with "Leadership Conference 1980" and highlights of 1979-80 description in black. Attendee's name and title is imprinted in black lettering (example: John Cooke). 4 1/8" high x 3 1/2" diameter at top with indented base at bottom. $20.00-25.00

GI8028

❑ **GI8029 Indianapolis Region Mug.** Indianapolis region cream colored coffee mug with gold rim. Mug is inscribed "McDonald's Indianapolis Region" in black and personalized with recipient's name on back in black. Same message as on the 1980 Leadership Conference Mug. 4" high x 3 1/2" diameter. $10.00-20.00

❑ **GI8030 Milwaukee Region Glass Stein.** McDonald's and Milwaukee logo in black on the front of the stein. On the back in yellow and black graphics is a Milwaukee scene and symbols of sports teams. $10.00-15.00

❑ **GI8031 25th Anniversary Ronald McDonald House Mug.** White ceramic mug decorated with accomplishments of the last twenty-five years as well as Ray Kroc and the upcoming Olympics. $40.00-50.00

GI8031 (shown from two sides)

❑ **GI8032 Breakfast Heating Up Coffee Mug.** White ceramic mug with orange graphics depicting "Breakfast is sizzlin' Heat it Up!" $5.00-8.00

❑ **GI8033 Breakfast Brigade Clear Mug.** Clear glass mug painted white on inside with McDonald's logo in gold (red or rust colored logos). No Breakfast logo. Underneath logo are the words, "breakfast brigade" in black. On bottom of mug is "D-99." Each $5.00-8.00

GI8033

❑ **GI8034 Christmas Coffee Mug.** Christmas 1980 cream colored, pottery coffee mug. McDonald's logo in red and green with "Christmas 1980" in green. $5.00-8.00

❑ **GI8035 Hook 'Em Horns Glass.** University of Texas clear pedestal base glass with cartoon mascot imprinted with "Hook 'em Horns" in orange lettering. $35.00-50.00

❑ **GI8036 Hook 'Em Horns Glass Austin, Texas.** University of Texas clear pedestal base glass with cartoon mascot imprinted with "Hook 'em Horns" in dark orange lettering and Austin, Texas imprint on back of glass. $35.00-50.00

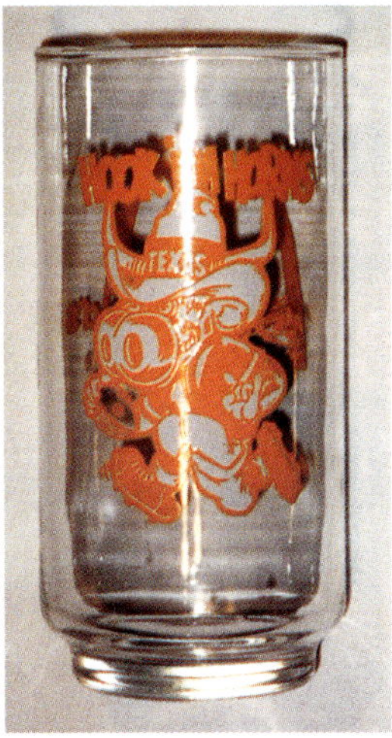

GI8035

GI8036

GI8036 (back)

❑ **GI8037 New Orleans Saints Glass.** Round bottom glass with NFL logo on back and Saints helmet logo on the front. Coke logo is imprinted on one side with McDonald's logo on the other. Graphics are in black, gold and white with zebra stripes in gold and black around the glass. 5 1/4" high. $10.00-15.00

❑ **GI8038 Baylor Bears Glass.** Clear pedestal base glass with cartoon of Baylor Bear and McDonald's logo on one side. Logo is in green. $35.00-50.00

GI8037

GI8038

❑ **GI8039 Baylor Bears Glass with Waco Texas.** Clear pedestal base glass with cartoon of Baylor Bear and McDonald's logo on one side. Logo is in green with Waco, Texas imprint in green. $35.00-50.00

❑ **GI8040 Daisy Glass.** Wide mouth glass with pedestal base imprinted around the center of the glass with a band of yellow and white daisies with red centers. Below flower imprint is a band of yellow arches and McDonald's logo. 3 1/2" high. $3.00-5.00

❑ **GI8041 Arches Old Fashioned Glass.** Clear glass with a line of arches around the top of the glass. $5.00-10.00

GI8038-39

GI8040

GI8041

❑ **GI8042 McDonald's Seniors Coffee Mug.** Cream colored coffee mug inscribed with "Congratulations McDonald's seniors 1980" in red. 5" high x 3 1/4" diameter at top and 3 5/8" diameter at base. $5.00-8.00

❑ **GI8043 Fall River Mug.** Fall River, Massachusetts ceramic white pottery mug imprinted "25th Anniversary 44 Wm. S. Canning Blvd, Fall River, Mass. 1/3/62" in red. McDonald's logo is imprinted in red on the back of the mug. $5.00-10.00

Hawaii Glasses (4"), 1980s

❑ **GI8044 Fisherman bringing in nets.** $5.00-8.00

❑ **GI8045 Sunset with catamaran.** $5.00-8.00

GI8044-47

❑ **GI8046 Outrigger racers with people.** $5.00-8.00

❑ **GI8047 Surfing.** $5.00-8.00

Comments: Smoked glass set of four glasses came with a box and, in some cases, a map of Hawaii. Designs were etched on the glasses. 4" high.

GI8101-04

Box for GI8044-47

1981

• **"You Deserve A Break Today" theme repeated**

The Great Muppet Caper Glasses (5 3/4"), 1981

Muppet Character Glasses:

❑ **GI8101 Happiness Hotel.** $1.00-1.50

❑ **GI8102 Kermit on a bike.** $1.00-1.50

❑ **GI8103 Kermit with Fozzie in a gondola.** $1.00-1.50

❑ **GI8104 Miss Piggy.** $1.00-1.50

Comments: The Great Muppet Caper Promotion was a huge promotion for McDonald's! The set involved four glasses, display, hanging dangler, trayliner, paper badge worn by employees, and window advertising, as well as posters and assorted regional advertising. Due to overexposure, the price of the vast amount of glasses on the market has remained very low. Glasses celebrated the release of *The Muppet Caper* movie.

The Great Muppet Caper glasses display.

The Great Muppet Caper glasses translite.

The Great Muppet Caper glasses employee badge.

The Great Muppet Caper glasses trayliner.

The Great Muppet Caper Convention Glasses (5 3/4"), 1981

Muppet Character Convention Glasses:

- ❑ **GI8105 Happiness Hotel with GOLD lining.** $250.00-400.00
- ❑ **GI8106 Kermit on a bike with GOLD lining.** $250.00-400.00
- ❑ **GI8107 Kermit with Fozzie in a gondola with GOLD lining.** $250.00-400.00
- ❑ **GI8108 Miss Piggy with GOLD lining.** $250.00-400.00

Comments: The Great Muppet Caper Convention Promotion was only for a select number of McDonald's employees. Two sets of these glasses are known to exist. Price is only an estimate of future auction activity. Glasses are lined with a gold color.

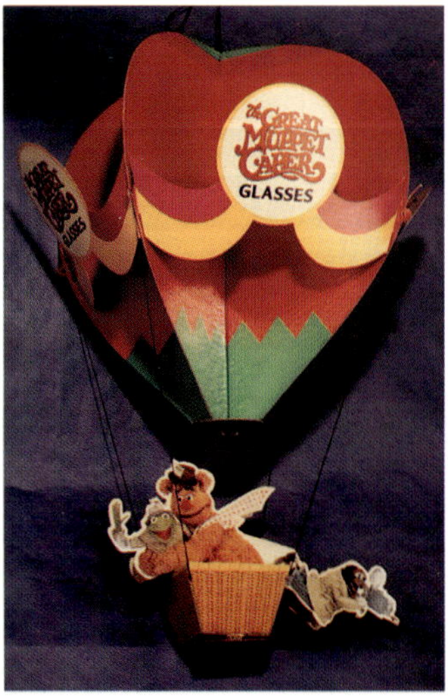

The Great Muppet Caper glasses dangler.

GI8105-08

Generic Glasses and Mugs, 1981

❑ **GI8109 Muppet Caper Manager's Glass.** Muppet Caper Manager's Glass was inscribed with the commitment date: February 2, 1981 announcing that "Extra! The Muppets are Coming!" to one's local McDonald's. Graphics are white with Miss Piggy riding a motor scooter on the front and Gonzo taking a FLASH picture on the back. Few were sent to store management announcing the upcoming glass promotion. $350.00-450.00

GI8109 (shown from three sides)

❑ **GI8110 Denver Region Coffee Mug.** White ceramic mug with multicolored Christmas wreath graphics and "Seasons Greetings Denver Region 1981" in black on the front of the mug. 3 1/4" high x 3 1/2" diameter. $5.00-8.00

❑ **GI8111 Albany Region Wine Glass.** Clear wine glass is from Albany, New York region marked in gold lettering on location and McDonald's arches. 8.5" high. $15.00-20.00

❑ **GI8112 Amelia Island Wine Glass.** Wine glass has McDonald's logo in black and yellow with catamaran graphics and "1981 Amelia Island" in black lettering. 7" high. $15.00-20.00

❑ **GI8113 Agency Co-op Meeting Coffee Mug.** Cream colored ceramic coffee mug has McDonald's breakfast logo and "Agency Convention 1981" in black on the front. "I'm Giving Breakfast the Business" is in black on the mug's back. $5.00-8.00

❑ **GI8114 Christmas 1981 Mug.** Clear colored mug with McDonald's logo and "Christmas 1981" imprinted in red. $10.00-15.00

GI8111

GI8114

❑ **GI8115 Personnel/Labor Relations Metal Cup.** Metal coffee cup has red graphics with "1981 (Be Daring Logo) Personnel / Labor Relations" inscribed. 2 1/2" high x 3 5/8". $5.00-8.00

❑ **GI8116 Communication Services Mug.** Brownish, cream colored ceramic coffee mug with tan graphics. McDonald's logo and "Communication Services The Best Communication Services Group in the World" imprinted on the front of the mug. "Thanks for Everything. Your Friends at Lidejo Sales Promotional Agency" and Lidejo logo imprinted on the back of the mug. "Staffordshire Kilm Made in England" imprinted on the bottom. $10.00-15.00

❑ **GI8117 Christmas Champagne Glass.** Designed for 1981 Las Vegas convention. Glass is clear, pedestal style with green outline of a Christmas tree, red Christmas balls on tree, and black outlined Ronald. Inscription reads, "Ronald places arches on top of tree." Paper disc marked, "Margaritaville, San Diego Region." $35.00-65.00

GI8117

1982

- **7th National Owners Operators Convention**

Place: San Francisco, California
Theme: "One of a Kind"

- **Ray Kroc's 80th Birthday Celebration**

Generic Glasses and Mugs, 1982

❑ **GI8201 San Francisco Owners Operators Stein.** Clear glass stein inscribed with "San Francisco 1982" etched on the front. Given out at the Owners Operators convention in San Francisco, California. 5 1/2" high x 3 1/4" diameter at the top and 4 1/2" diameter at the base. $20.00-25.00

❑ **GI8202 Personnel Wine Glass.** Balloon style wine glass given out at the 1982 San Francisco Owners Operators Convention at Personnel booth. Imprinted with "Progressive Professional Leadership Personnel" in red lettering. 8.5" high x 3 1/8" diameter at top. $10.00-15.00

❑ **GI8203 International Accounting Meeting Glass Stein.** International McDonald's log with "International Accounting Chicago 1982" in red, yellow, and black lettering. Additionally, "World Cup Champions of Accounting & Business" imprinted in black on the back of the stein. Indented base. 5 5/8" high x 2 1/4" diameter at top.
$10.00-15.00

❑ **GI8204 Michigan Glass Stein.** Heavy glass stein imprinted with "1982 Managers Con-

vention Dearborn, Michigan" in black with McDonald's logo in black on the back.
$10.00-15.00

❑ **GI8205 Ronald McDonald House Glass Stein.** White ceramic stein with "Ronald McDonald House" logo in black and red; inscribed with "The House That Love built" in black on the back. $10.00-15.00

❑ **GI8206 Ronald Sitting Shoe Mug.** White ceramic mug depicting Ronald sitting cross legged, hand to face. On the back of the mug is McDonald's logo in a red square. Underside of mug is embossed "Staffordshire, England / Kilmcraft." 3.5" high.
$10.00-20.00

❑ **GI8207 Ronald McDonald Show Mug.** White ceramic mug with imprints of Ronald's red shoe encircling the mug. Mug was sold in McDonald's Gift Shops for a number of years. 12 oz. $3.00- 4.00

❑ **GI8208 Ronald McDonald Shoe Rock Drink Glass.** Clear glass etched with picture of Ronald McDonald's shoe. 10 oz.
$5.00-7.00

❑ **GI8209 Ronald McDonald Shoe Beverage Drink Glass.** Clear glass etched with picture of Ronald McDonald's shoe. 12 oz.
$5.00-7.00

❑ **GI8210 McDonald's Arches Tankard.** Clear tankard etched with arches. 13 oz.
$10.00-15.00

❑ **GI8211 Crystal Rocks Glass.** Bubble in glass, crystal glass etched with initials monogram and arches encircling the top of the glass. 10 oz. $10.00-15.00

❑ **GI8212 Crystal Beverage Glass.** Bubble in glass, crystal beverage glass etched with initials monogram and arches encircling the top of the glass. 12 oz. $10.00-15.00

❑ **GI8213 Crystal Beverage Mug.** Bubble in glass, crystal beverage mug etched with initials monogram and arches encircling the top of the mug. 14 oz. $10.00-15.00

❑ **GI8214 Knoxville World's Fair Glass / Small printing.** Flared, clear glass with white band encircling the glass. Imprinted with "The 1982 World's Fair May-October 1982 Knoxville, Tennessee USA" with the "O" in the lettering being the globe. On the back of the glass is the description of "Energy Turns the World." One glass has the whole month spelled out on the front of the glass, e.g. "October 1982...," while the second type has only the year visible on the front of the glass. Differences are due to promotion mold settings. $5.00-6.00

GI8214

Left: GI8215; Right: GI8214

Reverse sides of GI8214 and GI8215 are the same.

❑ **GI8215 Knoxville World's Fair Glass / Large printing.** Flared clear glass with white band encircling the glass. Imprinted with "The 1982 World's Fair May-October 1982 Knoxville, Tennessee USA" with the "O" in the lettering being the globe. On the back of the glass is the description of "Energy Turns the World." One glass has the whole month spelled out on the front of the glass, e.g. "October 1982...," while the second type has only the year visible on the front of the glass. Differences are due to promotion mold settings. $5.00-6.00

❑ **GI8216 Ronald McDonald Shoe Tankard.** Clear tankard etched with picture of Ronald McDonald's shoe. 14 oz. $10.00-20.00

❑ **GI8217 Ronald Mug.** White porcelain mug with red rim has Ronald with hands by face on front and back of mug. McDonald's logo is in yellow and black. Imprinted on bottom of mug is "Ronald McDonald and McDonald's Corporation 1982 Porcelain made in Korea." 3 1/2" high x 3 1/4" wide. $5.00-8.00

❑ **GI8218 Ronald House Mug.** Brown ceramic mug with gold metallic graphics. Ronald House, RMCC logo on the front and "Everyday another child says thanks. Ronald McDonald Dinner-Dance October 1982" on back. $4.00-5.00

❑ **GI8231 Old Fashioned Beverage Glass.** Smoke colored glass with "McDonald's" and arches on front of the glass in gold. $5.00-10.00

GI8231

Milwaukee Brewers - McDonald's Sports Glasses, 1982

❑	**GI8219 Fingers/Simmons.**	$5.00-7.00
❑	**GI8220 Yount/Ogilvie.**	$5.00-7.00
❑	**GI8221 Molitor/Vuckovich.**	$5.00-7.00
❑	**GI8222 Thomas/Cooper.**	$5.00-7.00

Comments: The Milwaukee Brewers sold four glasses in this series in 1982. Two Brewers players were pictured on each glass made by the Libbey Glass Company in black, yellow, and blue. Players Robin Yount, Ben Ogilvie, Gorman Thomas, Cecil Cooper, Paul Molitor, Pete Vuckovich, Rollie Fingers, and Ted Simmons are pictured on the glasses. 5 5/8" high.

GI8219-20

Pittsburgh Steelers All Time Greatest - McDonald's Sports Glasses, 1982

❑	**GI8223 Blount.**	$5.00-7.00
❑	**GI8224 Gerela.**	$5.00-7.00
❑	**GI8225 Greene.**	$5.00-7.00
❑	**GI8226 Mullins.**	$5.00-7.00

Comments: The Pittsburgh Steelers series consisted of four glasses, heavy high ball type glasses and/or beverage glasses. Graphics were imprinted in black, brown, white, and yellow with two names and pictures per glass and the McDonald's logo on each glass.

GI8223-24

GI8223-26

World Cup Soccer Glasses, 1982

- ❑ **GI8227 Players riding on the bus.** $35.00-50.00
- ❑ **GI8228 Players celebrating on the field.** $50.00-60.00
- ❑ **GI8229 Crown in the stands.** $35.00-50.00
- ❑ **GI8230 Men holding flags running.** $35.00-50.00

Comments: Set of four glasses was distributed in Spain during the World Cup Soccer event in 1982.

GI8227-30

1983

- **7,000th Store Opening in Falls Church, Virginia**

McDonaldland Action Embossed Arches Series IV, 1983

McDonald's Character Glasses:

- ❑ **GI8301 Big Mac on roller skates with embossed "M".** $50.00-75.00
- ❑ **GI8302 Grimace with pogo stick with embossed "M".** $50.00-75.00
- ❑ **GI8303 Hamburglar on flat car with embossed "M".** $50.00-75.00
- ❑ **GI8304 Ronald playing leapfrog with embossed "M".** $75.00-100.00

GI8301-04

Comments: Regional distribution: Southern California. Glasses have raised "M" arches circling bottom rim of glass and arches on bottom of glass. They are marked: "© 1983 McDonald's Corp." These glasses were also distributed in Singapore in 1983 with promotional danglers and counter cards. California cases of embossed arches glasses could have originated from leftover Singapore promotion. 5 5/8" high.

Camp Snoopy Collection Glasses, 1983

- ❑ **GI8305 Rats! Why is having fun so much work?** $2.00-4.00
- ❑ **GI8306 The struggle for security is no picnic.** $2.00-4.00
- ❑ **GI8307 There's no excuse for not being properly prepared.** $2.00-4.00
- ❑ **GI8308 Civilization is overrated.** $2.00-4.00
- ❑ **GI8309 Morning people are hard to love.** $3.00-4.00

- ❑ **GI8322 Camp Snoopy Manager's Glass.** "Good Grief! McDonald's Camp Snoopy Glasses are Coming!" Sent to selected managers announcing the Camp Snoopy Glass promotion. $250.00-500.00

Comments: Glass size is 6" high with the glasses sold individually and/or packaged in sets of four, making the fifth glass ("Morning People Are Hard to Love") a little more difficult to collect. The series also came in white plastic cups, to be discussed in a future book. 6" high.

GI8305-09

Get your
LUCY
glass this week!
THERE'S NO EXCUSE FOR NOT BEING PROPERLY PREPARED

Get your
LINUS
glass this week!
THE STRUGGLE FOR SECURITY IS NO PICNIC!

Get your
WOODSTOCK
glass this week!
BLAAT!

Get your
SNOOPY
glass this week!
CIVILIZATION IS OVERRATED!

Camp Snoopy glasses translite.

Camp Snoopy glasses translite.

Blue book for Camp Snoopy glass promotion.

Blue book for Camp Snoopy glass promotion (inside).

Camp Snoopy glasses crew badge.

Boxed set of Camp Snoopy glasses.

Camp Snoopy glasses, set of four.

Camp Snoopy glasses trayliners.

Blue book for Camp Snoopy glasses.

Houston Livestock Show and Rodeo Glasses, 1983

- ❑ **GI8310 Bareback Bronco Riding / Saddle.** $5.00-6.00
- ❑ **GI8311 Women's Barrel Racing / Chuckwagon Races.** $5.00-6.00
- ❑ **GI8312 Clown / Calf Scramble.** $5.00-6.00
- ❑ **GI8313 Bull Riding / Steer Wrestling.** $5.00-8.00

Comments: Glasses are marked with the "McDonald's Arches" logo and marked, "McDonald's Collector Series 1983, First, Second, Third or Fourth in a Series of Four. 1983 McDonald's Corporation." Each glass depicts two different designs.

GI8310-13

GI8310-13, with McDonald's logo.

Generic Glasses and Mugs, 1983

❑ **GI8314 St. Louis Champagne Glass.** Short, pedestal fluted champagne glass has McDonald's logo and "Welcome to the Showboat Region Managers Convention 1983" in red on a steam boat graphic on the front of the glass. 6 1/2" high. $15.00-20.00

❑ **GI8315 Franklin Part, Illinois Glass Stein.** Stein is root beer style with "Franklin Part, IL" imprinted in red and yellow on the front. Store address and phone numbers were added for the regional store distribution. $10.00-20.00

❑ **GI8316 Chicago Region Glass Stein.** Amber colored glass stein has the Chicago Region logo and "Operations Training" in white print on the front of the stein. $15.00-25.00

GI8316 (third from left)

❑ **GI8317 Chicago Region Wine Glass.** Clear wine glass has McDonald's logo etched on the front. 6 1/4" high. $15.00-20.00

❑ **GI8318 Chicago Region Glass Stein.** Glass stein has "Security 1983" etched on the front with the Chicago logo graphics. $10.00-20.00

❑ **GI8319 My Chicken's McChicken Mug.** White ceramic mug imprinted with "My Chicken's McChicken." $5.00-8.00

GI8319

❑ **GI8320 International Hamburglar Catching a Ride Glass.** Hamburglar is featured on a clear glass with colored graphics. Glass is marked in Japanese and has the arches encircling the bottom of the glass. One in a series of at least two to four. $25.00-50.00

❑ **GI8321 International Mayor McCheese Sailing Glass.** Mayor McCheese is featured on a clear glass with colored graphics. Glass is marked in Japanese and has the arches encircling the bottom of the glass. One in a series of at least two to four. $25.00-50.00

GI8320

GI8321

1984

- **8th National Owners Operators Convention**

  Place: Los Angeles and San Diego, California (Jack Murphy Stadium - San Diego)
  Event: Convention + Ray Kroc's 80th Birthday party
  Theme: "Delivering the Difference"

- **8,000th Store Opening in Duluth, Georgia,** commemorated with a glass peach

- **50 Billion Hamburgers Sold Celebration**

Houston Livestock Show and Rodeo Glasses, 1984

- ❑ **GI8401 Bareback Riding / Saddle Bronc Riding.** $5.00-8.00
- ❑ **GI8402 Women's Barrel Racing / Chuckwagon.** $5.00-8.00
- ❑ **GI8403 Cutting Horses / Calf Scramble.** $5.00-8.00
- ❑ **GI8404 Steer Wresting / Bull Riding.** $5.00-10.00

Comments: Glasses have the "McDonald's Arches" logo and are marked, "McDonald's Collector Series 1984, First, Second, Third or Fourth in a Series of Four ©1984 McDonald's Corporation." Each glass depicts two different designs.

GI8401-04

Olympic Mugs, 1984

- ❑ **GI8405 Baseball, Volleyball, Basketball, Soccer.** White outline. $4.00-5.00
- ❑ **GI8406 Sailing, Kayaking, Sculling, Swimming.** Blue outline. $4.00-5.00
- ❑ **GI8407 Steeplechase, Fencing, Ice Skating, Cycling.** Red outline. $4.00-5.00
- ❑ **GI8408 Wrestling, Track, Archery, Weight Lifting.** Yellow outline. $4.00-5.00

GI8405-08

Olympic Manager's Glass, 1984

❑ **GI8409 Olympics 1984 Manager's Glass.** "See me in action on 4 exciting Olympic glasses!" $250.00-500.00

Olympic Prototype Glasses, 1984

❑ **GI8410 Sam Swimming.** $250.00-500.00
❑ **GI8411 Sam Soccer.** $——
❑ **GI8412 Sam Track.** $——
❑ **GI8413 Sam Gymnastics.** $——
❑ **GI8414 Sam, The Mascot.** $250.00-500.00

Comments: Olympic mugs have sports illustrations on their clear glass front with the Olympic logo and McDonald's logo illustrated in gold and blue on the reverse side. They are imprinted with "1984 Olympics" in red, blue, yellow, or white on the front.

A Manager's Glass advertised the glasses to the stores. A limited number of store owners received this advertising glass. In addition, a very limited number of glasses were produced before the glasses were cancelled. Plastic cups replaced the glasses, which were made of relatively thin glass. The Manager's glass reads "See me in action on 4 exciting Olympic glasses."

The known samples of the prototype glasses are Sam the Eagle Swimming/Diving and Sam The Mascot. Commitment date for the set was November 1, 1983, when the Manager's glass was sent to the selected stores. The price range on the prototype glasses has doubled the range on private sales. The additional three prototype glasses are presumed to exist.

GI8409 (shown from three sides)

GI8410 (front)

GI8410 (back)

GI8414

Generic Glasses and Mugs, 1984

❑ **GI8415 Christmas 1984 Mug.** Clear colored mug with McDonald's logo and "Christmas 1984" imprinted in red along with regional store address. $10.00-15.00

GI8415

❏ **GI8416 Merry Christmas 1984 Mug.** Clear colored mug with McDonald's logo and "Merry Christmas 1984" imprinted in red along with regional store address (McDonald's of Newark, New York). $10.00-15.00

❏ **GI8417 50 Billion Celebration Wine Glass.** Clear wine glass with "50,000,000,000 Celebration" and McDonald's arches in white. $15.00-20.00

❏ **GI8418 Delivering the Difference Stein.** Dark blue ceramic stein printed with "Delivering the Difference" plus McDonald's arches in gold on the front. Stein was given out at the Los Angeles Owner Operator Convention. A Canadian version was also manufactured. 5" high and 3" diameter at top. $15.00-20.00

GI8416

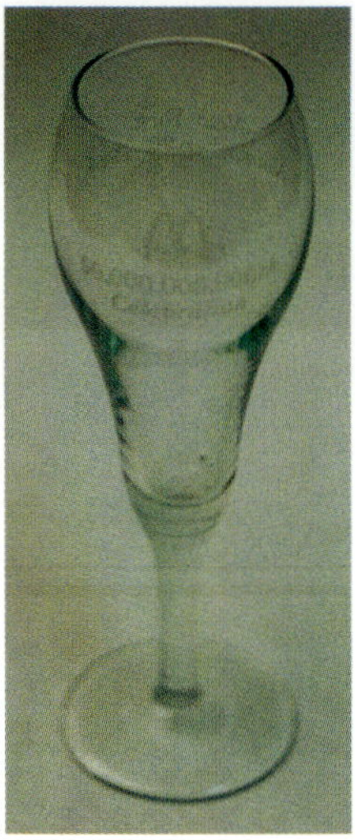

GI8417

GI8418 (Canadian version on left, USA version on right)

❏ **GI8419 Hamburger University Class 200 Stein.** Large ceramic cream colored stein with McDonald's Hamburger University logo in gold and black with a gold rim. Imprinted with "Class 200" and Hamburger University logo in black. $15.00-20.00

❏ **GI8420 Hamburger University Professor Stein.** Large ceramic cream colored stein with McDonald's Hamburger University logo in gold and black with a gold rim. Imprinted with "Professor" and Hamburger University logo in black. $15.00-20.00

GI8420

❑ **GI8421 Hamburger University Senior Professor Stein.** Large ceramic cream colored stein with McDonald's Hamburger University logo in gold and black with a gold rim. Imprinted with "Senior Professor" and Hamburger University logo in black. $15.00-20.00

❑ **GI8422 Ronald Olympic Glass.** Clear glass with Ronald's head featured on the front of the glass with a yellow band above and below the figure pose. On the back is the Olympic logo and "Los Angeles 1984 Olympics" imprinted in black. Glass has an indented base with raised arches around the base. McDonald's logo is imprinted in raised font on the bottom of the glass. 6" x 2 1/4" x 3 1/4" $——

❑ **GI8423 Golden State Food Supplier Mug.** White ceramic mug with "Golden State Foods Corporation..." imprinted in black on the back of mug and Ronald under a tree with a child in a swing on the front. $5.00-8.00

GI8423 (front)

GI8423 (back)

❑ **GI8424 Olympic Mug Without Figures.** White ceramic mug with Olympic logo on front, no gold figures down the side. Inscribed "Helping Olympic Dreams Come True." 10 oz. $4.00-6.00

❑ **GI8425 Olympic Mug With Figures.** White ceramic mug with Olympic logo on front and gold color figures down the sides. Inscribed "Helping Olympic Dreams Come True." 10 oz. $5.00-8.00

❑ **GI8426 Olympic Mug Without Figures.** White ceramic mug in larger size with Olympic logo on front, no gold figures down the side. Inscribed "Helping Olympic Dreams Come True." 16 oz. $5.00-8.00

GI8424

GI8425

GI8426

❑ **GI8427 I Support Ronald McDonald House Mug.** White ceramic mug with Ronald McDonald house characterization on front plus sun in right hand corner. 10 oz. $2.00-4.00

❑ **GI8428 My Morning Mug.** White ceramic mug with "My Morning Mug" in yellow printing, round handle. 10 oz. $2.00-4.00

❑ **GI8429 My Morning Mug.** White ceramic mug with "My Morning Mug" in orange printing, rectangular handle. 10 oz. $2.00-4.00

GI8528-29

❑ **GI8430 "We're here when you need us" Mug.** White ceramic mug with "We're here when you need us" imprinted in red under the yellow arches. 10 oz. $2.00-3.00

❑ **GI8431 Ronald McDonald Children's Charities Mug.** White ceramic mug with Ronald holding children's hand and imprinted with "Ronald McDonald Children' s Charities / Established in memory of Ray A. Kroc." $2.00-4.00

GI8430

GI8431

❑ **GI8432 International France Wine Glass.** Wine glass is imprinted with PARIS / January 23, 1984. $20.00-25.00

GI8432

❑ **GI8433 International Hong Kong Good Morning Cup.** Porcelain cup has yellow arches with a large smiling sun behind the arches highlighting the phrase, "Good Mornings Start At McDonald's." The phrase is in English with Chinese writing beneath the jingle. Cup is dated 1984 McDonald's Corp. $7.00-10.00

❑ **GI8434 St. Petersburg Wine Glass.** Clear wine glass imprinted with "St. Petersburg Region 1984" and McDonald's arches in gold with gold rim. $15.00-20.00

GI8433

GI8434

1985

- **30th Year Celebration**

Generic Glasses and Mugs, 1985

❑ **GI8501 30th Year Celebration Mug.** Large white ceramic mug highlighting the events of the last thirty years. $25.00-45.00

GI8501 (shown from three sides)

❑ **GI8502 30th Year Celebration Mug.** Clear glass mug with "McDonald's 30th Anniversary" imprinted in black and yellow along with the logos used for the last thirty years on the front of the mug. 3 1/2" high x 3" diameter at top. $7.00-10.00

❑ **GI8503 30th Year 1985 Birthday Mug.** Clear glass mug with silvertone imprint, "1985 Birthday" on the front, 30th and McDonald's logo imprinted on the back. $5.00-8.00

GI8502

GI8503

❑ **GI8504 Hamburger University Time Capsule Dedication Stein.** Large ceramic cream colored stein with McDonald's Hamburger University logo in gold and black and a gold rim. Imprinted with "Time Capsule Dedication April 15, 1985" and Hamburger University logo in black. $15.00-20.00

❑ **GI8505 Taste Panel Mug.** Black ceramic mug with silver color coating and McDonald's logo on one side. "Taste Panel 1985" etched on the front. 3 3/4" x 3". $4.00-7.00

❑ **GI8506 Kansas City Regional Mug.** Cream colored ceramic mug with "Kansas City Region April 15, 1985" in red on the front and McDonald's 30th Year logo in red and black on the back. Also on the back is Speedee Sign with "April 15, 1955" in black print. When the mug is filled with a hot beverage, the old style red and white restaurant appears beside the sign. $20.00-25.00

❑ **GI8507 East Hanover, New Jersey Mug.** White ceramic mug with raised dark gray McDonald's restaurant graphic on the front and "Celebrating Thirty Years with You" imprint on the back. Additionally, "East Hanover, New Jersey April 15, 1985" is imprinted in a raised gray front style. $5.00-8.00

❑ **GI8508 Chesaning, Michigan Mug.** Clear glass pedestal mug with "Show Boat City" imprinted on the front and paddlewheel graphics on the back. $5.00-10.00

GI8508

❑ **GI8509 Allegan, Michigan Mug.** Clear glass pedestal mug with "Allegan, MI 1985" imprinted on the front. $5.00-10.00

❑ **GI8510 NBMOA Convention 1985.** Gray ceramic coffee mug for the National Black McDonald's Operators Association Convention in 1985. Gray mug had a gold rim and the Atlanta skyline in black around the imprint of "NBMOA." "1985 National Convention Atlanta" appears in gold with light gray horizontal lines around the top. On the back in gold color is former Sr. Executive Vice President Gerry Newman's signature. On the bottom, "Made in England" appears in raised letters. $50.00-75.00

GI8511

GI8510

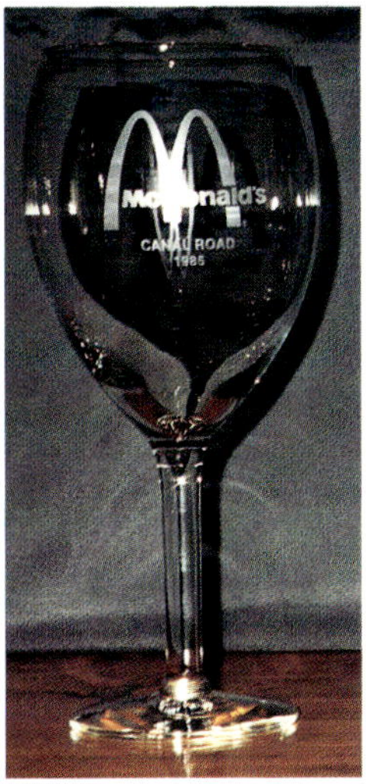

GI8512

❑ **GI8511 Northland Drive Wine Glass.** Balloon style wine glass with "Christmas Fiesta at McDonald's, Northland Dr. Dec 1985" imprinted on the front of the clear glass. $10.00-20.00

❑ **GI8512 Canal Road Wine Glass.** Large balloon style wine glass with "Canal Road 1985" imprinted on the front of the clear glass. $10.00-20.00

❑ **GI8513 Hamburger University Time Capsule Dedication Stein.** Large ceramic stein in cream color with McDonald's Hamburger University logo in black and gold and "Time Capsule Dedication April 15, 1985" in black on the front. $15.00-25.00

GI8513

❑ **GI8514 International Big Mac Kinder Mug.** Big Mac holding McDonald's flag on a white colored mug with the arches encircling the bottom of the mug. $25.00-35.00

❑ **GI8515 International Mayor Kinder Mug.** Mayor McCheese holding McDonald's flag on a white colored mug with the arches encircling the bottom of the mug.
$25.00-35.00

GI8514-15

❑ **GI8516 International Ronald Kinder Mug.** Ronald on a white colored mug with the arches encircling the bottom of the mug.
$25.00-35.00

GI8516

1986

• **9th National Owners Operators Convention**

Place: Las Vegas, Nevada
Theme: "Back To Our Future"

McVote Glasses (6"), 1986

❑ **GI8602 Big Mac - No one else stacks up.** $8.00-10.00
❑ **GI8603 McDLT for burger of the year.** $8.00-10.00
❑ **GI8604 Quarter Pounder with cheese in '86.** $8.00-10.00

Comments: Free McVote glasses were distributed in regional areas to determine the strength of particular burger choices.

McVote '86
McVote '86
ALL THE MAKINGS OF A WINNER
McVote '86
HE'S THE BIG CHEESE IN BURGERS

GI8602-04

McVote '86
McVote '86
HE'S THE BIG CHEESE IN BURGERS
McVote '86
ALL THE MAKINGS OF A WINNER

McVote '86
BALLOT BOOK
COUPONS IN BACK
McDonald's
FREE McVOTE '86 GLASS
Come to McDonald's, cast your vote and receive your free commemorative McVote '86 glass.* There are three in all, each representing one of the three candidates. Collect all three of these limited edition glasses, (retail value over $3.00).
So come to McDonald's and be a part of McVote '86. Your vote will make a difference in deciding, who will be Burger of the Year.
*with purchase of Big Mac, McD.L.T. or Quarter Pounder with Cheese and large french fries.

Garfield Mugs #1, 1986

Garfield Checkered Mugs:

- ❑ **GI8605 Blue Checkered:** Whoever invented evenings... $5.00-7.00
- ❑ **GI8606 Yellow Checkered:** The early cat gets... $5.00-7.00
- ❑ **GI8607 Red Checkered:** I've never seen a sunrise... $5.00-7.00
- ❑ **GI8608 Green Checkered:** I never met a dinner... $5.00-7.00

Comments: Mugs were test marketed in Pennsylvania. Two phrases appear on each checkered mug. The success of this promotion led to the national promotion the end of the year. 3 1/2" high.

GI8605-08

Garfield Mugs #2, 1987 / 1986

Garfield Clear Mugs:

- ❑ **GI8609 I'm easy to get along with...** $.50-1.00
- ❑ **GI8610 I'm not one who rises...** $.50-1.00
- ❑ **GI8611 It's not a pretty life...** $.50-1.00
- ❑ **GI8612 Use your friends wisely.** $.50-1.00

Comments: Due to popular demand from the set that was test marketed earlier in the year, this second set was distributed on a massive scale. The amount of mugs produced, however, exceeded the demand. This over-distribution resulted in a common price of ten to twenty-five cents for these mugs in excellent condition. They are cute and easily obtained. 3 1/2" high.

GI8609-12

Garfield Mugs #2 translite.

Garfield Mugs #2 counter card.

Garfield Mugs #2 trayliner.

Garfield Mugs #3, 1986

- ❑ **GI8613 Garfield with mustache up...** $3.00-5.00
- ❑ **GI8614 Garfield with full set of teeth...** $3.00-5.00
- ❑ **GI8615 Garfield with mustache down...** $3.00-5.00

Comments: This series of three Garfield mugs was distributed by Group II through their catalogue. The mugs are not marked with McDonald's logo; they are a generic Garfield style used in Garfield Sweepstakes in the stores. 3 1/2" high.

GI8613-15

Generic Glasses and Mugs, 1986

- ❑ **GI8616 Ronald's Shoe Mug.** White ceramic mug with red shoe imprint encircling the mug in four layers. $3.00-5.00
- ❑ **GI8617 Scrabble Mug.** White ceramic mug with Scrabble™ game design on the front of the mug. $3.00-5.00

GI8616

GI8617

❑ **GI8618 Chicago Bears High Ball Glass.** Commemorates Super Bowl XX Chicago Bears. High Ball glass has Chicago Bears and McDonald's logo in blue and orange on clear glass with imprint, "Super Bowl XX January 26, 1986 Louis Superdome New Orleans" in orange. $20.00-35.00

GI8619

❑ **GI8619 Fort Worth, Texas Wine Glass.** Clear wine glass is marked, "Hullen Mall - Fort Worth, Texas." $20.00-25.00

❑ **GI8620 Breakfast Co-Op 1986 Glass.** Clear glass with box design McDonald's logo in gold, red, and black. On the bottom of the glass is the imprint, "U.S.A." 3 3/4" high. $5.00-15.00

❑ **GI8621 International 100th Store Opening Japan Mug.** Gray ceramic beer mug features Ronald graphics and "100" along with the McDonald's logo. $15.00-20.00

GI8622

❑ **GI8622 International Character Mug.** Ronald, Hamburglar, and Big Mac riding a bicycle built for three are featured on this cream colored mug from the Philippines. $20.00-35.00

❑ **GI8623 9th National Owners Operators Convention Champagne Glass.** Crystal etched champagne glass with McDonald's logo and "Las Vegas 1986" etched on the front. 8 1/4" high x 1 3/4" diameter at top. $15.00-25.00

GI8623

1987

Generic Glasses and Mugs, 1987

❑ **GI8701 Priority One Stein.** Clear, heavy glass pedestal stein with pewter medallion on the front featuring the Golden Arches and "Priority One." Stein was given out at the Combined Operations meeting in 1987. 5" high x 3 1/2" diameter at top. $15.00-25.00

GI8701

❑ **GI8702 Hamburger University 30,000 Student Stein.** Stein is a large cream colored ceramic stein with McDonald's Hamburger University logo in gold and black with the imprint, "30,000th Student" and "Class 390 January 12-22, 1987" on the back of the stein. $15.00-20.00

❑ **GI8703 Hamburger University Stein.** Cream colored stein with the basic Hamburger University logo in black. $10.00-15.00

❑ **GI8704 Everything Under the Sun Cup.** White ceramic cup with yellow smiling sun at the top, followed by the imprint, "We've got everything under the sun" in purple. Also displayed is the McDonald's logo in gold. $3.00-5.00

❑ **GI8705 McDonald's Logo Mug.** Clear glass tankard mug with red and yellow McDonald's logo and store address on the front. $3.00-5.00

❑ **GI8706 Big Mac Coffee Mug.** White ceramic coffee mug has the graphics, "Big Mac Under Glass" in gold and black line art drawing. Also displayed is the "GSF" Golden State Foods logo in gold from a Big Mac sandwich (in gold) on a plate marked, "Hawaii 1987." The same design is repeated on the back. Mug was issued by Golden State Foods (a McDonald's supplier) in connection with their RMCC Ronald McDonald Children's Charity fundraiser. $4.00-5.00

❑ **GI8707 McDonald's Script Mug.** Ceramic mug in black, white, or blue with the McDonald's logo scripted in red on white, white on lavender, gold on black, or red on yellow. 12 oz. $3.00-5.00

GI8707

❑ **GI8708 McDonald's Arches Mug.** White ceramic mug with the arches forming a border around the bottom of the mug, 1" from the base. $3.00-5.00

❑ **GI8709 Much Too Early Mug.** White ceramic mug with the imprint, "Much Too Early to Start Talking" on the side. $2.00-3.00

❑ **GI8710 Gone For the Morning Mug.** White ceramic mug with the imprint, "Gone For the Morning" on the side. $2.00-3.00

❑ **GI8711 While You Were Out Mug.** White ceramic mug with the imprint, "While You Were Out Mug" on the side. $2.00-3.00

❑ **GI8712 Warning: First Cup Mug.** White ceramic mug with the imprint, "Warning: First Cup" on the side. $2.00-3.00

❑ **GI8713 Washington D.C. Mug.** White ceramic mug with the imprint, "McDonald's Corp. Washington D.C." on the side. $2.00-3.00

❑ **GI8714 Dark Blue Tankard.** Dark blue tankard with the McDonald's logo inscribed in gold. $10.00-15.00

❑ **GI8715 International Canada Celebrating 20 Years Mug.** Cream colored mug with red Maple Leaf graphics and yellow arches. $5.00-8.00

GI8714

GI8715

GI8708

❑ **GI8716 International Canada Water Glass.** Clear water glass on pedestal base with Canadian Maple Leaf logo. $10.00-15.00

❑ **GI8717 International Canada Liquor Decanter and Highball Glasses.** Clear highball glasses with Canadian Maple Leaf logo and clear glass decanter. Set $50.00-75.00

❑ **GI8718 International Canada Tall Drink Glass.** Tall frosted glass with yellow lines encircling the top and bottom of the glass, McDonald's logo in yellow on front. $8.00-10.00

GI8716

GI8717

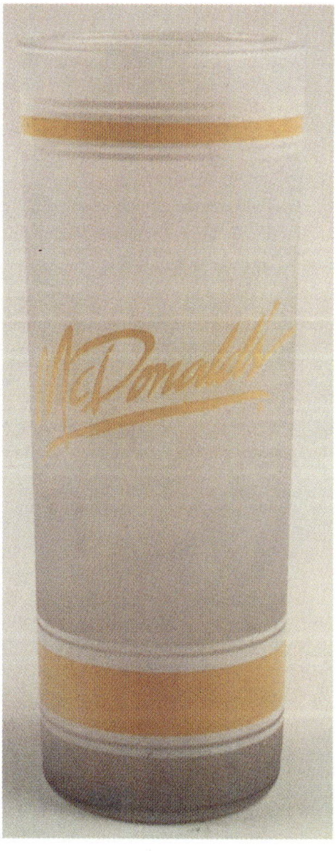

GI8718

❑ **GI8719 International Canada Highball Glass.** Highball frosted glass with yellow lines encircling the top and bottom of the glass, McDonald's logo in yellow on front. $8.00-10.00

❑ **GI8720 International Canada Coffee Mug.** White mug with the Canadian Maple Leaf logo, rectangular handle. $3.00-5.00

❑ **GI8721 4th Quarter Marketing Review Mug.** White ceramic mug with the imprint, "4th Quarter Marketing Review" on the side. $2.00-3.00

GI8719

International Canada Walt Disney Glasses, 1987

Disney glasses:
❑ **GI8722 Snow White.** $15.00-25.00
❑ **GI8723 Peter Pan.** $15.00-25.00
❑ **GI8724 Cinderella.** $15.00-25.00
❑ **GI8725 Mickey Fantasia.** $15.00-25.00

Comments: Set of four glasses promoted the introductions of the Disney Classics on video. Each glass is marked with the McDonald's logo.

GI8720

GI8722-25

Button promoting Canada's Disney glasses.

Disney button in French.

1988

- **10th National Owners Operators Convention**
- **10,000th Store Opening**

  Place: Washington, D.C.
  Theme: "Sharing the Dream"

Mac Tonight Promotions, 1988

GI8804-08

- ❑ **GI8804 Mac Tonight Juice Glass.** Clear glass with cityscape graphics. 6 oz. 4" high. $7.00-10.00
- ❑ **GI8805 Mac Tonight Drink Glass.** Clear glass with cityscape graphics. 8 oz. 5 1/4" high $7.00-10.00
- ❑ **GI8806 Mac Tonight Tumbler.** Clear glass with cityscape graphics. 14 oz. 6" high. $10.00-15.00
- ❑ **GI8807 Mac Tonight Storage Glass with Lid.** Clear glass with cityscape graphics. Double rocks glass was sold in grocery stores and gift shops. Came with a dark blue lid. 6 3/8" high. $15.00-25.00
- ❑ **GI8808 Mac Tonight Super Size Glass.** Clear glass with tapered sides with cityscape graphics. Marked, "DS0100GC © McDonald's Corporation 1988" on underside. 32 oz. 7" high. $15.00-25.00

❑ **GI8809 Mac Tonight Mug.** Tall, dark blue mug with Mac Tonight's head and "Make it Mac Tonight" in a boxed design with McDonald's logo on the front. $7.00-10.00

❑ **GI8810 Mac Tonight Piano Mug.** Dark blue coffee mug with "1988 McDonald's Corp." in white on side of mug. Illustrates a free floating key board with Mac Tonight playing. Marked, "Mac tonight" on front and back and "Button Up" in white beside the handle. $7.00-10.00

❑ **GI8811 Make It Mac Tonight Mug.** Dark blue ceramic coffee mug with Mac Tonight's head in gray and light blue. "Make It" in white and "Mac Tonight" in yellow on front and back. "Button Up" beside the handle. $7.00-10.00

❑ **GI8812 Mac Tonight Holding Mike Mug.** Dark blue ceramic coffee mug with Mac Tonight's head and hands holding microphone. Mac Tonight is wearing a red bow tie and "Mac Tonight" is in yellow. "Button Up" beside the handle. $7.00-10.00

GI8812

GI8811

Garfield Glasses, 1988

❑ **GI8813 Are we having fun yet?** $7.00-10.00

❑ **GI8814 Home, James.** $12.00-16.00

❑ **GI8815 Just me and the road.** $7.00-10.00

❑ **GI8816 Poetry in motion.** $7.00-10.00

Comments: Garfield glasses came in a set of four and were issued on a regional basis. 6" high.

GI8813-16

Garfield crew button.

GI8802

Generic Glasses and Mugs, 1988

❑ **GI8801 10,000th Store Grand Opening Champagne Glass.** "Owner / Operator Convention April 5-9, 1988 - Washington D..C." etched into the clear champagne glass. $15.00-20.00

❑ **GI8802 10,000th Store Rock N Roll Mug.** Clear heavy mug with a jukebox imprinted in red on the front and "McDonald's Potomac Mills." The back has the bisected arches in red. $5.00-8.00

GI8801

GI8801 boxed set.

❑ **GI8803 10,000th Store Fluted Champagne Glass.** Clear fluted champagne glass etched with, "Official Toasting Glass McDonald's 10,000th Restaurant Dale City, Virginia USA April 6, 1988" on back and McDonald's logo on front. Came in a presentation box with bottle of champagne. 8 1/4" x 2" diameter at top. $15.00-20.00

❑ **GI8817 Good Times Great Taste Stein.** Clear glass stein with McDonald's logo and "It's a Good Time for the Great Taste" etched on the front. $10.00-20.00

❑ **GI8818 Good Times Great Taste Coffee Mug.** Milk glass coffee mug with yellow McDonald's breakfast logo. On top in yellow is inscribed, "It's A Good Time" and "For The Great Taste." Additionally, "North 5th & G Streets" is in yellow. On the back in red is "U.S. Marines MCAS El Toro." 3 1/4" high. $5.00-8.00

GI8803 reverse side.

GI8803

❑ **GI8819 American Cup Mug.** Black ceramic mug inscribed with "1988 McDonald's American Cup...U.S. Gymnastics Federation." $4.00-7.00

❑ **GI8820 Olympic Mug.** White ceramic mug with red and gold Olympic logo in wave design. $4.00-5.00

❑ **GI8821 Serving Kansas Mug.** Clear glass mug with McDonald's logo and "Serving Kansas 25 years" etched on the front. $5.00-8.00

❑ **GI8822 St. Mary of Nazareth Mug.** Pedestal glass coffee mug with red and yellow McDonald's logo and gold graphic of St. Mary. Inscribed "Saint Mary of Nazareth Hospital Center" on back in yellow. 5 1/4" high x 2 4/5" diameter at top and 2 1/2" diameter at base. $7.00-10.00

❑ **GI8823 Kansas City Stein.** White ceramic stein commemorating 1988 Kansas City Assistant Managers Convention, with "Kansas City" imprinted in red and McDonald's logo in gold. 4 3/4" high. $15.00-20.00

❑ **GI8824 San Diego Champagne Glass.** Long stemmed champagne glass with McDonald's logo and "San Diego Region Grand Opening December 2, 1988" etched on the front. $10.00-15.00

GI8824

❑ **GI8825 Raleigh Region Highball Glass.** Clear highball glass with etched poinsettia design around the McDonald's logo, inscribed, "Raleigh Region 1988." $15.00-25.00

❑ **GI8829 Fraggle Rock Mug.** Cream colored mug features four Fraggle Rock characters (pictured on page 63 of *McDonald's Happy Meal Toys Around the World* book). $5.00-7.00

❑ **GI8834 International Canada Drink Coca-Cola Classic Glass.** Clear glass with red, black, and yellow stained glass appearance with McDonald's Canadian logo on front. $5.00-8.00

GI8819

GI8834

Toledo Zoo Panda Mugs, 1988

- ❑ **GI8826 Nan-Nan.** $5.00-7.00
- ❑ **GI8827 Le-Le.** $5.00-7.00
- ❑ **GI8828 Pandas.** $5.00-7.00

Comments: The Toledo Zoo sold a series of three mugs featuring the Panda Bears' history. McDonald's logo and Panda picture on each clear glass mug.

GI8826-28

International Philippines Good Times, Great Taste Mugs, 1988

Character Mugs:

- ❑ **GI8830 Grimace.** $20.00-25.00
- ❑ **GI8831 Ronald.** $20.00-25.00
- ❑ **GI8832 Birdie.** $20.00-25.00
- ❑ **GI8833 Hamburglar.** $20.00-25.00

Comments: White ceramic mugs are marked with, "Good Times Great Taste" on the underside.

GI8830-33

International McDonaldland Character Glasses, 1988

Character Glasses:

- ❑ **GI8835 Birdie flying.** $5.00-8.00
- ❑ **GI8836 Hamburglar walking with hamburger.** $5.00-8.00
- ❑ **GI8837 Grimace batting.** $5.00-8.00
- ❑ **GI8838 Ronald forming Magic Arch.** $5.00-8.00

Comments: Set of four glasses from Canada advertised the characters to Canadian McDonald's patrons.

GI8835-38

International McDonaldland character glasses translite.

Comments: This series of four glasses was a regional promotion, tested in St. Louis. Two different designs appear on each glass along with a descriptive paragraph. Marked with "1989 McDonald's Corp. / 1989 The Walt Disney Company" logos. 5 1/2" high.

Disneyland glasses translite.

1989

- **11,000th McDonald's Opens in Hong Kong (October 20th)**

McDonald's Salutes Disneyland Glasses, 1989

- ❑ **GI8901 Goofy in Adventureland.** $8.00-10.00
- ❑ **GI8902 Donald in Critter Country.** $8.00-10.00
- ❑ **GI8903 Minnie in Fantasyland.** $8.00-10.00
- ❑ **GI8904 Mickey in Tomorrowland.** $8.00-10.00

GI8901-04

Disneyland glasses trayliner.

Generic Glasses and Mugs, 1989

❑ **GI8905 BMOA Wine Glass.** Clear wine glass with Black McDonald's Operators Three Points of Unity etched on front and "National Black McDonald's Operators Association Biennial Convention Long Beach, CA October 17-21, 1989" etched on the back. 6" x 2" x 2 4/5" $25.00-40.00

❑ **GI8906 Agency Co-Op Shot Glass.** Small shot glass with "1989 Co-op Presidents Advertising Agency Convention" printed in blue on the back. Cowboy graphics and "Performance Concepts" in blue on the front. $10.00-15.00

❑ **GI8907 My Morning Mug.** White ironstone coffee mug with white interior and more traditional rounded handles. In the early eighties, the mugs had fancy "teacup" and rectangular type handles. From 1989 through 1999, McDonald's sold rounded handle morning mugs with white lining. They came in two McDonald's logo colors, red and dark orange. They came with "breakfast brigade" printing, with and without the sun logo in upper right hand corner. Over supply has decreased the price to under one dollar in many regional areas. Each is 3 3/4" high. $1.00-3.00

GI8907 (color variations without sun logo)

Top: GI8907 (with sun logo)

GI8909

- ❑ **GI8908 Happy Holidays Mug.** White ceramic mug with Christmas tree branch on front of mug in green and red Christmas ball printed with "Happy Holidays" and McDonald's logo in red on front and back. $3.00-5.00

- ❑ **GI8909 Class of '89 Mug.** Black Hamburger University Mug with white printing. $2.00-3.00

- ❑ **GI8913 Corporate Stein.** Corporate legal stein made from milk glass with dark green graphics. Pictures three wise men representing Shelby Yastrow, Burt Cohen, and George Rummel, all employees of the Corporate Legal Department, along with a camel and star. Stein was given out to department employees during the 1989 Christmas party. McDonald's logo is on one of the kings. 5" high x 3 1/8" diameter at top x 3 7/8" diameter at base. $10.00-20.00

- ❑ **GI8914 Martin Luther King Mug.** Brown ceramic coffee mug with Martin Luther King and candle graphics in gold. McDonald's logo imprinted with gold along with the message, "The ultimate message of man is not where he stands in moments of comfort and convenience, but where he stands at times of Challenge & Controversy" in gold on back. $75.00-100.00

International Coffee Mugs, 1989

- ❑ **GI8910 French Roast coffee.** $4.00-5.00
- ❑ **GI8911 Irish Creme coffee.** $4.00-5.00
- ❑ **GI8912 Vienna Roast coffee.** $4.00-5.00

Comments: Black ceramic mugs came with coffee packets, in some regional areas of Pennsylvania.

GI8910-12

GI8910

International Coffee Mugs crew button.

The Nineties

1990

- **35th Anniversary of McDonald's**
- **11th National Owners Operators Convention**

Place: Las Vegas, Nevada
Date: May 7-11, 1990
Theme: "Call to Action, Customer Satisfaction"

35th Anniversary button.

Pittsburgh Steelers Hall of Fame Sports Glasses, 1990

- ❑ **GI9001 1st of 4 - Steeler's Players.** $4.00-5.00
- ❑ **GI9002 2nd of 4 - Steeler's Players.** $4.00-5.00
- ❑ **GI9003 3rd of 4 - Steeler's Players.** $4.00-5.00
- ❑ **GI9004 4th of 4 - Steeler's Players.** $4.00-5.00

Comments: Glasses are tall, heavy glasses with black, yellow, and white graphics and imprint. Back of glass is numbered in the series of four glasses and lists McDonald's logo as well as TV stations. 6 1/4" tall.

GI9001-04

Pittsburgh Steelers Hall of Fame glasses translite.

Generic Glasses and Mugs, 1990

- ❑ **GI9005 Communication Service Stein.** Glass stein with indented base. Black graphics of a monk with a camera and the phrase, "We're Still the One." Imprinted with Communication Service logo. 5 1/2" high x 2 7/8" diameter top x 2 1/4" diameter at base. $5.00-15.00

- ❑ **GI9006 Brandy Snifter.** Brandy snifter from Flint, Michigan imprinted with, "Linden Rd., Flint Michigan August 29, 1990." $35.00-50.00

- ❑ **GI9007 I Support Ronald McDonald House.** White ceramic mug with five color graphic imprint, "I Support Ronald House" in black. Mugs may have been issued earlier and repeated through the years. $3.00-5.00

- ❑ **GI9008 Replica Coffee Mug.** White ceramic mug holds 9 oz. with a handle. Graphics are the same as the Styrofoam cup of the 1990 era with McDonald's logo and three bands of arches in yellow, orange, and rust encircling the cup. Listed in Group II catalogue as Group II product. $2.00-4.00

GI9006

GI9008

❑ **GI9009 McDonald's Logo Mug.** Ceramic mug holds 12 oz. with a row of arches around the base of the mug in gold and "McDonald's" in large script on the front. Mugs came in gold imprint on black or cobalt blue or black on gray. $3.00-5.00

❑ **GI9010 Signature McDonald's Mug.** Ceramic mug holds 12 oz. with "McDonald's" in large script in gold on black, gold on cobalt blue, black on gray, royal on white, red on black, yellow on red, black on gold, pink on black, red on white, or lavender on white. $3.00-5.00

❑ **GI9011 Signature McDonald's Mug.** Ceramic mug holds 15 oz. with "McDonald's" in large script in bone on royal or royal on gold. $3.00-5.00

❑ **GI9012 Broadway 160 NYC Champagne Glass.** Champagne glass with grand piano graphics and "160 Broadway" in gold. 8 1/2" high x 1 1/4" diameter top x 2 5/8" diameter at base. $7.00-15.00

❑ **GI9013 Broadway 160 NYC Highball Glass.** Highball glass with a gold rim and "160 Broadway" in gold. $7.00-10.00

❑ **GI9014 Broadway 160 NYC Mug.** Mug with a gold rim and "160 Broadway" in gold and piano graphics etched in the front. $7.00-10.00

❑ **GI9015 Broadway 160 NYC Mac Tonight Mug.** Blue ceramic mug with Mac Tonight graphics and "McDonald's 160 Broadway NY" in gold. $7.00-10.00

❑ **GI9016 Broadway 160 Shot Glass.** Clear shot glass with piano graphics in black. $7.00-10.00

❑ **GI9017 Jar Mug.** Clear glass mug holds 16 oz. with white screw cap. Has McDonald's logo and restaurant address in black. $2.00-4.00

❑ **GI9018 Together, McDonald's and You Champagne Glass.** Clear champagne glass with "Together, McDonald's and You" in red imprinted on the front. 4 1/2" x 3 1/8". $5.00-8.00

❑ **GI9019 Ronald House Stein.** Clear glass stein with blue graphics of Ronald McDonald House and "Ronald McDonald House Buffalo, NY" imprinted in blue on the front. 5 5/8" x 2 7/8". $7.00-15.00

❑ **GI9020 Michael Jordan RMCC Mug.** White ceramic coffee mug with graphics and imprint, "Michael Jordan and RMCC Celebrity Golf Championship. Benefiting RMCC and Michael Jordan Foundation." $20.00-25.00

❑ **GI9021 Lidejo Convention Mug.** White ceramic coffee mug in dark gray with convention and promotion graphics, "I love (heart) McDonald's Conventions." Marked on bottom, "China." 3 3/4" x 3". $3.00-5.00

❑ **GI9022 McDonald's Stein.** Gray ceramic stein holds .5 liters with yellow and black McDonald's logo in black banded box. 5" x 3 1/8". $4.00-8.00

❑ **GI9023 Free Enterprise Stein.** Clear stein with, "McDonald's Maintaining Your Free Enterprise" imprinted in red. 5 1/2" x 3" x 3 3/8". Imprinted on the bottom with "L". $5.00-8.00

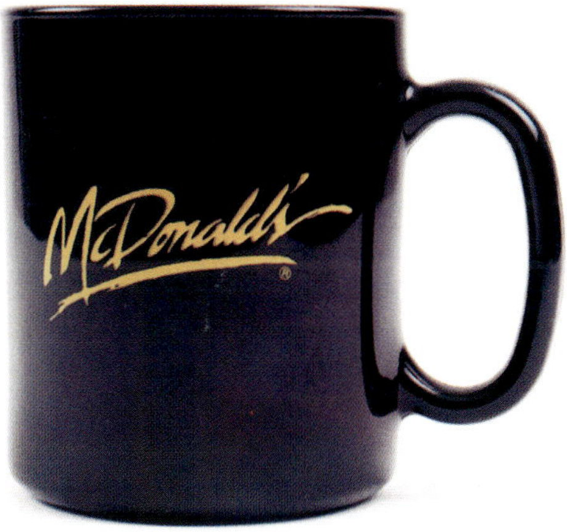

GI9010

❑ **GI9024 International Canada McDonald's Shot Glass.** Clear shot glass with McDonald's Canadian logo. $4.00-8.00

GI9024

❑ **GI9025 Regional Store Mug.** Clear mug with imprint of store address and year in red. McDonald's logo is in red with arches in gold. $4.00-8.00

❑ **GI9030 International Japan Disney Donald Glass.** Clear glass with Donald and a magnifying glass. Japanese writing and McDonald's arches on the glass and on the pink box. One of a set of two or three glasses. $50.00-75.00

❑ **GI9031 International Japan Disney Mickey Mouse Glass.** Clear glass with Mickey's portrayal in Fantasia. Japanese writing and McDonald's arches on the glass and the pink box. A third glass is presumed to exist. $50.00-75.00

GI9030-31

Box for GI9030

GI9025

GI9030-31

❑ **GI9032 International Australian Coca-Cola Glass.** Clear glass like the USA glass except "Drink Coca Cola" is in red and black on the leaded glass effect design and the McDonald's Australian logo is in black and yellow on the glass. Indented foot glass. 5 5/8" x 2 3/4". $15.00-25.00

GI9032

❑ **GI9033 International Brazil Espresso Cup.** White ceramic espresso cup with red rim. McDonald's logo is imprinted on the red box style logo with "Sao Paulo" in black and "Nicholas Lanas Barrios" on bottom. 2 1/4" tall x 1 7/8" wide at top rim. $10.00-15.00

❑ **GI9034 International Miniature German Stein.** Blue and white ceramic stein with pewter lid. "M Muchen" is engraved on the lid. 3" x 3 3/8". $5.00-10.00

Nutcracker Glasses, 1990

❑ **GI9026 Marie receives Nutcracker.** $6.00-8.00

❑ **GI9027 Marie and Prince in Toyland.** $6.00-8.00

❑ **GI9028 Sugar Plum Fairy.** Castle, swan, boat. $6.00-8.00

❑ **GI9029 Nutcracker battles Mouse King.** Decorated Christmas tree. $6.00-8.00

GI9026-29

Comments: Nutcracker series of four glasses was a regional promotion in 1990. Top and bottom edges had white bands with green holly and red berries. On one side is a scene from the *Nutcracker* musical; the other side has a quote from the story in black and McDonald's logo. Marked, "Copyright 1990 McDonald's Corporation." Nutcracker glasses came FREE or were sold for .79 cents with purchase of a $5.00 gift certificate booklet in regional areas.

Nutcracker glasses register topper.

International Mugs, 1990

- ❑ **GI9035 Wolkje.** $5.00-8.00
- ❑ **GI9036 Zwart.** $5.00-8.00
- ❑ **GI9037 Veeel.** $5.00-8.00
- ❑ **GI9038 N' Koffie.** $5.00-8.00

Comments: Four white ceramic mugs are marked in black with various phrases and McDonald's logo.

GI9035-38

1991

- **12,000th Store Opening in New Hyde Park, New York (March 22th)**

Generic Glasses and Mugs, 1991

❑ **GI9101 DeWitt, Michigan Goblet.** Mercury lined glass goblet imprinted with "DeWitt, MI January 21, 1991." $10.00-20.00

GI9101

❑ **GI9102 Regional Store Mug.** White milk glass mug with store address imprint in red and red arches. $1.00-2.00

❑ **GI9103 Season's Greeting Mug.** Red ceramic mug has Rudolph with arches incorporated into his antlers. Mug holds 11 oz. $3.00-5.00

GI9103

GI9102

1992

- **12th National Owners Operators Convention**

Place: Orlando, Florida
(Orange County Convention Center)
Theme: "Together we've got what it takes"

Generic Glasses and Mugs, 1992

❑ **GI9201 Convention Skyline Glasses.** Clear engraved water glasses with matching water pitcher served as convention gifts. Set of four glasses had the McDonald's logo and the Orlando, Florida skyline etched in the glass. One glass $5.00-10.00

GI9201

❑ **GI9202 Regional Greenville Convention Wine Glass.** Clear stemmed wine glass from Managers Regional Convention in Greenville, North Carolina. Etched wine glass was imprinted with "Convention 1992." $15.00-25.00

GI9202

❑ **GI9203 Middletown Coffee Mug.** Ceramic mug imprinted with "McDonald's celebrates 25 Years - The Nation's Largest Seller of Hamburgers February 21, 1992. 149 West Main Road, Middletown" in red on white. $3.00-5.00

❑ **GI9204 Heart Shaped Mug.** Corporate, heart shaped mug has "Thanks from the bottom of our heart!" imprinted in red with McDonald's logo on white ceramic mug. $3.00-5.00

❑ **GI9205 Red Wing Pottery Coffee Mug.** Red Wing, Minnesota stoneware coffee cup with Red Wings as logo along with McDonald's logo, dated 1992. $5.00-8.00

International Canada Character Mugs, 1992

Character Mugs:

❑ **GI9206 Ronald.** $3.00-5.00
❑ **GI9207 Hamburglar.** $3.00-5.00
❑ **GI9208 Grimace.** $3.00-5.00
❑ **GI9209 Birdie.** $3.00-5.00

Comments: Set of four white ceramic mugs were issued in Canada in 1992 to selected employees and managers.

GI9206-09

1993

• **McWorld promoted**

GI9301-4

Nostalgia Historical Classics Glasses I, 1993

❑ **GI9301 I'm Speedee and Arches.** $8.00-10.00

❑ **GI9302 McDonald's Restaurant Circa 1957.** $5.00-8.00

❑ **GI9303 The Original Shake, Burger & Fries.** $5.00-8.00

❑ **GI9304 Speedee Service System.** $5.00-8.00

Comments: The set of four clear Classic Glasses were sold for .99 cents in parts of Ohio and Pennsylvania. They are a tapered "Coca Cola" style glass with red, blue, and yellow graphics. Copyright is imprinted on each glass along with the important date: 1993. This original set is much more difficult to obtain then the later set, dated 1995. 6" high.

Generic Glasses and Mugs, 1993

❑ **GI9305 Seasons Greetings Mug.** White ceramic mug with McDonald's restaurant address in red and green on 11 oz mug. $3.00-4.00

❑ **GI9306 Marque Mug.** Yellow ceramic coffee mug imprinted with nineties style new arch logo over the box style logo in red. 11 oz. $2.00-3.00

❑ **GI9307 International Classic Mug.** Dark gray, 11 oz. ceramic coffee mug has three color logo: triangle with circle "International Classic" overlaid, "McDonald's" logo overlaid on the "International Classic" design. Colors imprinted are light gray, pink, and light blue. $2.00-4.00

❑ **GI9308 Hut Stricklin and #27 Racing Car Stein.** White ceramic stein comes with a colored decal, dated 1993. Stein was sold by Classic Crafts in Tennessee. $5.00-8.00

❑ **GI9309 Hut Stricklin and #27 Racing Glass.** Clear ceramic glass comes with a colored decal, dated 1993. Glass was sold by Classic Crafts in Tennessee. $2.00-5.00

❑ **GI9310 Hut Stricklin and #27 Mug.** Ceramic coffee cup comes with a colored decal, dated 1993. Mug was sold by Classic Crafts in Tennessee. $2.00-5.00

❑ **GI9311 Hunter Team Hut Stricklin and #27 Mug.** White ceramic coffee cup comes with a colored decal, dated 1993. Mug was licensed by NASCAR. $2.00-5.00

❑ **GI9312 Hunter Team Hut Stricklin and #27 Racing Car Stein.** White ceramic stein comes with a colored decal, dated 1993. Stein was licensed by NASCAR. $5.00-8.00

❑ **GI9313 Hunter Team Hut Stricklin and #27 Racing Car Mason Jar.** Clear, handled mason jar was a pint size glass mug. Product was licensed by NASCAR. $2.00-3.00

❑ **GI9314 Jurassic Park Mug.** Gray Jurassic Park mug with the Jurassic Park logo. $2.00-4.00

GI9314

❑ **GI9315 Good Morning Mug.** Reissued Good Morning mug has the box style logo. Comes in white ironstone with sun in the upper right hand corner of the logo. $1.00-2.00

❑ **GI9316 First Class Stamp Mug.** Gray ceramic mug comes with Ronald Stamp design in red. $2.00-4.00

GI9316

Philadelphia Phillies / New Orleans Saints Baseball Team Logo Glasses, 1993

Team Logo Glasses:

❑ **GI9317 New Orleans Zubaz Design.** $8.00-12.00

❑ **GI9318 Phillies Zubaz Curve Design.** $2.00-3.00

❑ **GI9319 Phillies Zubaz Stripe Design.** $2.00-3.00

Comments: Phillies design glass set of two were sold in the Philadelphia area. Glasses highlight McDonald's logo and Coke logo with the Liberty Bell featured on the front of each Phillies glass. The New Orleans Saints glass is imprinted in gold and black with the team's helmet logo on the front and McDonald's logo on the side. 5 5/8" high.

GI9317-19

GI9317-19

All Time Greatest Team / MLB Trading Card Glasses, 1993

Baseball Players:

- ❑ **GI9321 Johnny Bench.** $6.00-8.00
- ❑ **GI9322 Roberto Clemente.** $6.00-8.00
- ❑ **GI9323 Lou Gehrig.** $6.00-8.00
- ❑ **GI9324 Willie Mays.** $6.00-8.00
- ❑ **GI9325 Joe Morgan.** $6.00-8.00
- ❑ **GI9326 Cal Ripken.** $7.00-10.00
- ❑ **GI9327 Brooks Robinson.** $6.00-8.00
- ❑ **GI9328 Babe Ruth.** $6.00-8.00
- ❑ **GI9329 Nolan Ryan.** $6.00-8.00
- ❑ **GI9330 Carl Yastzremski.** $10.00-25.00

Comment: Original set of nine glasses was sold in the Washington D.C. area. Clear glasses were reproductions of TOPPS baseball trading cards with each player's signature and statistics. Each glass had McDonald's logo, Coke logo, Major League Baseball, and TOPPS logos. 5 3/4" x 2 1/2" diameter at top. The tenth glass was only sold in the Boston area, representing the designated hitter.

Left: GI9328; Right: GI9330

Left: GI9329: Right: GI9321

Left: GI9323; Right: GI9325

Left: GI9326; Right: GI9327

Left: GI9322; Right: GI9324

International Hong Kong World of Fun Glasses, 1993

Character Glasses:

❑ **GI9331 Birdie dancing with flowers** $35.00-50.00

❑ **GI9332 Ronald dancing with headdress.** $35.00-50.00

❑ **GI9333 Grimace dancing with spear.** $35.00-50.00

❑ **GI9334 Hamburglar dancing with flag.** $35.00-50.00

Comments: Set of four McDonald's World of Fun glasses are clear glasses marked with McDonald's logo. Distributed May 4-June 6th in Hong Kong, Macau, and China.

GI9331-34

International Canada Character Glasses, 1993

Character Glasses:

❑ **GI9335 Grimace.** $10.00-15.00

❑ **GI9336 Ronald forming arches.** $10.00-15.00

❑ **GI9337 Hamburglar.** $10.00-15.00

❑ **GI9338 Birdie Flying.** $10.00-15.00

Comments: Set of four McDonald's Character glasses, originated in Canada.

GI9335-38

1994

- **1st Worldwide Owners Operators Convention**

Place: Las Vegas, Nevada (Hilton Convention Center)
Theme: "Great Expectations"

Generic Glasses and Mugs, 1994

❑ **GI9401 Great Expectations Wine Glass.** Solid crystal wine glass has the "Great Expectations" logo. $7.00-10.00

❑ **GI9402 MCN Mug.** Gray ceramic coffee mug has MCN logo in yellow, red, green, blue, and black with "McDonald's Communications Network" in red. Given out at the Las Vegas Owners Operators Convention. $5.00-8.00

GI9402

❑ **GI9403 Nostalgia Mug.** Bell shaped mug is made of stoneware and features the original McDonald's "Speedy" billboard with a single arch and the Coca-Cola logo on the back. 12 oz. $3.00-5.00

GI9403

❑ **GI9408 Flintstones "Roc Donald's" Mug.** Cream colored ceramic mug has red and yellow Roc Donald's logo and "Summer '94 A.D." in black. $2.00-4.00

GI9408

❑ **GI9409 McDonald's Collectors Club Mug.** White ceramic mug had the McDonald's Collectors Club logo on the front. $3.00-5.00

❑ **GI9410 Ronald Character Mug.** Ronald is featured with black sunglasses on a white ceramic mug. 11 oz. $3.00-5.00

GI9410

❑ **GI9421 International Canada Pizza Glass.** Tall clear glass with PIZZA logo formed on the bottom half of the glass. $3.00-5.00

GI9421

Customer Satisfaction Mugs, 1994

❑ **GI9404 "The McDonald's way is Customer Satisfaction."** $2.00-3.00
❑ **GI9405 "Whatever it Takes."** $2.00-3.00
❑ **GI9406 "Our Goal Taking Care of the McDonald's Customer."** $2.00-3.00
❑ **GI9407 "McDonald Rule One Customer Satisfaction."** $2.00-3.00

Comments: The 11 oz. white ceramic coffee mugs came in four patterns. The first had brown and yellow graphics, the second had a blue logo, the third had a red and blue imprint, and the fourth had green graphics.

Flintstones Bedrock Mugs, 1994

❑ **GI9411 Mammoth.** $3.00-5.00
❑ **GI9412 Rocky Road.** $3.00-5.00
❑ **GI9413 Pre-Dawn.** $3.00-5.00
❑ **GI9414 Treemendous.** $3.00-5.00

Comments: Flintstones set of four glass mugs was a national promotion. Molded stone age scenes decorated the mugs.

GI9411-14

Bedrock mugs translite.

World Cup Soccer Glasses, 1994

Soccer Players:

❑ **GI9415 Smidts and Grung.** $20.00-25.00

❑ **GI9416 Meved and Preud Homme.** $20.00-25.00

❑ **GI9417 Albert and Staelens.** $20.00-25.00

❑ **GI9418 Scifo and Degryse.** $20.00-25.00

❑ **GI9419 Nilis and Boffin.** $20.00-25.00

❑ **GI9420 Ver Der Elst and Van Himst.** $20.00-25.00

Comments: Set of six tall glasses was given out in Belgium. Pictured along with the players is the Red Devil Soccer Team, U.S. Dog Mascot, McDonald's logo, WCUSA 94 Logo, and Coke Logo. 6 1/2" high x 2 3/8" top diameter with straight sides.

GI9415-20

1995

- **Have You Had Your Break Today? jingle**

1995 Classic glasses display

1995 Classic glasses translite.

Nostalgia Historical Classic Glasses II, 1995

Classic Glasses:

- ❏ **GI9501 I'm Speedee and Arches** $2.00-4.00
- ❏ **GI9502 McDonald's Restaurant Circa 1957** $2.00-4.00
- ❏ **GI9503 The Original Shake, Burger & Fries** $2.00-4.00
- ❏ **GI9504 Speedee Service System** $2.00-4.00

Comments: Classic set of four glasses was exactly like the 1993 set except dated 1995.

Generic Glasses and Mugs, 1995

- ❏ **GI9505 Speedee Fantasy Glass.** Unauthorized version of fifties style water glass was produced by an overzealous designer. Glass was never officially distributed through the McDonald's stores. $——

GI9505

❑ **GI9506 Season's Greetings Grimace Mug.** Green ceramic mug featured Grimace on a sled in white graphics with McDonald's logo as the sled runners. $3.00-5.00

❑ **GI9507 Gotham City Special Mug.** White ceramic mug features Bill Elliott's car designed as the Batman vehicle. $5.00-8.00

❑ **GI9520 International Euro Mug.** Black ceramic mug with Euro Disney graphics. $4.00-7.00

GI9506

GI9507

GI9520

❑ **GI9529 Ronald Signature Mug.** White ceramic mug with Ronald's signature in red on yellow. $3.00-5.00

GI9529

❑ **GI9525 Ronald McDonald House Mug.** Ronald McDonald House logo in red apple design. $2.00-3.00

GI9525

❑ **GI9526 Ronald Walking with Birdie Mug.** White ceramic mug with character illustration on back. $2.00-4.00

❑ **GI9527 Ronald Sitting Mug.** White ceramic mug with a sitting Ronald illustrated on both sides. $2.00-4.00

GI9526-27

❑ **GI9528 International German Mug.** Cream colored ceramic mug with "Einfach gut früstücken" imprinted on side. $3.00-4.00

GI9528

Batman Gotham Mugs, 1995

- ❑ **GI9508 Batman.** $3.00-5.00
- ❑ **GI9509 Robin.** $3.00-5.00
- ❑ **GI9510 Riddler.** $3.00-5.00
- ❑ **GI9511 Two-Face.** $3.00-5.00

Comments: Set of four mugs was similar to the Flintstones Bedrock designed mugs. Each was clear with Gotham City graphics.

GI9508-11 (shown on translite)

Batman Gotham glasses display.

Batman Gotham glasses trayliner.

International Japan Mugs, 1995

- ❑ **GI9512 Ronald's Shoes.** $4.00-8.00
- ❑ **GI9513 Ronald's Signature.** $4.00-8.00
- ❑ **GI9514 Grimace Smiling.** $5.00-8.00
- ❑ **GI9515 Food Characters.** $5.00-8.00
- ❑ **GI9516 Ronald's Shoe with Soccer Ball.** $5.00-8.00

Comments: Assortments of mugs was given or sold to employees in Japan.

GI9512-16

International Japan Glasses, 1995

- ❑ **GI9517 Ronald's Shoes.** $4.00-8.00
- ❑ **GI9518 Food Characters.** $4.00-8.00
- ❑ **GI9519 Shake with Glasses.** $5.00-8.00

Comments: Assortments of glasses were given or sold to employees in Japan.

International Puerto Rico Christmas Celebration, 1995

Christmas Glasses:

- ❑ **GI9521 Melchor.** $10.00-12.00
- ❑ **GI9522 Los Tres Reyes Magos.** $10.00-12.00
- ❑ **GI9523 Baltasar.** $10.00-12.00
- ❑ **GI9524 Gaspar.** $10.00-12.00

Comments: Puerto Rico celebrated the 1995 Holiday Season with a series of four glasses sold at McDonald's.

GI9517-19

GI9521-23

1996

• **13th National Owner Operator Convention**

Place: New Orleans, Louisiana
Theme: "QSC and Me"

Walt Disney World 25th Anniversary Glasses, 1996

❑ **GI9601 Mickey.** $3.00-5.00
❑ **GI9602 Minnie.** $3.00-5.00
❑ **GI9603 Goofy.** $3.00-5.00
❑ **GI9604 Hollywood and Vine Disney Characters.** $3.00-5.00

Comments: Set of four glasses came with and without the McDonald's silver sticker. Clear glasses were marked with the Disney logo.

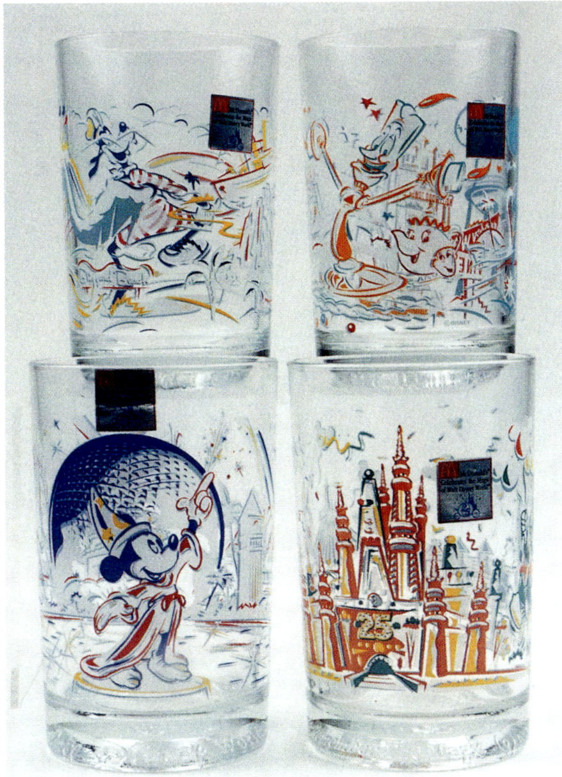

GI9601-04

Disney glasses register topper.

Olympic Glasses, 1996

- ❑ **GI9605 Olympic figure hurdling.** $10.00-20.00
- ❑ **GI9606 Olympic figure canoeing.** $10.00-20.00
- ❑ **GI9607 Olympic figure fencing.** $10.00-20.00

Comments: Olympic series of three glasses came with red, green, and yellow graphics. Glasses were distributed at special events at the Olympics by McDonald's and around the world at other special events.

GI9605-07

GI9605-07

Generic Glasses and Mugs, 1996

❑ **GI9608 Arches Mug.** Large goldtone arches appear on the cream colored mug with multi-colored "McDonald's" script. 11 oz. $3.00-5.00

❑ **GI9609 Halloween Mug.** White mug featured Happy Halloween graphics in orange and black with the McDonald's logo in orange. $3.00-4.00

❑ **GI9610 Hamburglar Candy Cane Mug.** Red ceramic mug features Hamburglar behind the arches. $3.00-4.00

❑ **GI9611 Speedee Mug.** Cream colored mug highlights Speedee and the fifties logo on the front. $3.00-5.00

❑ **GI9612 Packaging Graphics Mug.** Cream colored mug features McDonald's nineties style packaging logo. $2.00-3.00

GI9609

GI9608

GI9610

GI9611

GI9612

- ❑ **GI9613 Celebrating 25 Years Mug.** Mug celebrates twenty-five years in Vermont by McDonald's (started in 1971). $3.00-4.00

- ❑ **GI9614 Hamburglar Character Mug.** Black colored mug features Hamburglar' s nineties style graphics. $2.00-3.00

- ❑ **GI9615 Ronald Character Mug.** Red colored mug features Ronald's nineties style graphics. $2.00-3.00

- ❑ **GI9616 Grimace Character Mug.** Purple colored mug features Grimace's nineties style graphics. $2.00-4.00

GI9614-16

GI9615

❑ **GI9617 Globe Mug.** Clear international globe mug has the McDonald's logo imprinted on the back. $2.00-5.00

❑ **GI9618 Have You Had Your Break Today? Mug.** Ceramic mug features the nineties jingle. $2.00-3.00

GI9617

GI9618

❑ **GI9628 International Italian Coke Glass.** Clear Coke glass has Christmas greenery encircling the top of the glass. Marked with McDonald's Italy logo. $15.00-20.00

❑ **GI9629 International Canadian Decanter Glass.** Liquor glass with "McDonald's" spelled vertically along the side of the clear glass in yellow. $5.00-10.00

GI9628

GI9629

❑ **GI9635 International Japan Ronald Mug.** White mug with Ronald's face imprinted on the front and "I Love (Heart) Ronald" under the picture. $3.00-5.00

GI9635

❑ **GI9636 International Australia Logo Mug.** White ceramic mug with the McDonald's logo in green and green lines encircling the top and bottom of the mug. $3.00-5.00

GI9619-20

International Puerto Rico Olympic Celebration, 1996

Olympic Glasses:

❑ **GI9619 Baloncesto.** $10.00-12.00
❑ **GI9620 Fútbol.** $10.00-12.00
❑ **GI9621 Atletismo.** $10.00-12.00

Comments: Puerto Rico celebrated the 1996 Olympics with a series of three glasses sold at McDonald's. Some of these glasses were distributed at the Olympics in Atlanta to special McDonald's employees.

GI9636

GI9619; GI9621

International Italian McSports Collection Glasses, 1996

Sport Glasses:

❑ **GI9622 Soccer.** $20.00-25.00
❑ **GI9623 Archery.** $20.00-25.00
❑ **GI9624 Diving.** $20.00-25.00
❑ **GI9625 Baseball.** $20.00-25.00
❑ **GI9626 Basketball.** $20.00-25.00
❑ **GI9627 Marathon.** $20.00-25.00

Comments: Italy celebrated the Olympics with a series of six glasses.

GI9622-27

International Puerto Rico Christmas Celebration, 1996

Christmas Glasses:

❑ **GI9631 Star.** $10.00-12.00
❑ **GI9632 Three Kings.** $10.00-12.00
❑ **GI9633 One King.** $10.00-12.00
❑ **GI9634 Two Kings.** $10.00-12.00

Comments: Puerto Rico celebrated the 1996 Christmas season with a series of four glasses sold at McDonald's, similar to the 1995 Christmas promotion.

International New Zealand Hunchback of Notre Dame Mugs, 1996

Hunchback Mugs:

❑ **GI9637 Soldier with Shield.** $7.00-10.00
❑ **GI9638 Quasimoto.** $7.00-10.00
❑ **GI9639 Hugo.** $7.00-10.00
❑ **GI9640 Esmeralda.** $7.00-10.00

Comments: New Zealand celebrated the release of Disney's *The Hunchback of Notre Dame* movie with the issue of four clear heavy mugs.

GI9631-34

GI9637-40

1997

- **"My McDonald's" jingle**
- **"Did somebody say McDonald's?" jingle**

Generic Glasses and Mugs, 1997

❑ **GI9701 My McDonald's Mug.** Cream colored mug with nineties logo graphics in red, yellow and black. $2.00-3.00

❑ **GI9702 Ronald's Oval Shoe Mug.** Black colored oval base mug with Ronald's shoe imprinted in goldtone. $2.00-4.00

❑ **GI9703 Ronald's Shoe Mug.** Black colored standard mug with Ronald's shoe imprinted in goldtone. $2.00-4.00

GI9701

GI9702-03

❑ **GI9704 Splash Paint Mug.** Cream colored mug with nineties logo in a red box with paint splash in upper left corner of logo. $1.00-2.00

GI9704

❑ **GI9705 Coke Float Glass.** Clear colored coke glass was used with the Coke Float promotion. Glass is marked with Coke logo. $.25-.50

❑ **GI9706 Monopoly Glass Black and White.** Black and white line art Monopoly glass appears with black and white Monopoly board graphics. Glass was distributed in most of the United States as a game prize in the stores. McDonald's logo in white on the back. $4.00-10.00

GI9705

GI9705

❑ **GI9707 Monopoly Glass Colored.** Colored Monopoly glass appears with green, black, and red Monopoly board graphics. Glass was distributed in parts of West Virginia. McDonald's logo in yellow on the back. $10.00-15.00

GI9706-07 (front)

GI9706-07 (back)

Monopoly glass counter display.

❑ **GI9724 International Thailand Mug.** White frosted mug has multicolored arches encircling the front. $5.00-10.00

GI9724

International Belgium Glasses, 1997

Stella Artois Beer Glasses:

- ❑ **GI9708 Je T'ai Blesse.** $10.00-15.00
- ❑ **GI9709 Ben Je Gewond?** $10.00-15.00
- ❑ **GI9710 Blonde Comme Les.** $10.00-15.00
- ❑ **GI9711 Mooie KraagHeb Jij.** $10.00-15.00
- ❑ **GI9712 Et Si On.** $10.00-15.00
- ❑ **GI9713 Heb Jij Geen Dorst?** $10.00-15.00
- ❑ **GI9714 Zwelen We Samen.** $10.00-15.00
- ❑ **GI9715 T'as Pas Soif Toi?** $10.00-15.00

GI9708-09

GI9710-11

GI9712-15

GI9712-15 reverse side.

Jupiler Beer Glasses:

- ❑ **GI9716 Je Tai Blesse.** $10.00-15.00
- ❑ **GI9717 Ben Je Gewond.** $10.00-15.00
- ❑ **GI9718 Mooie KraagHeb Jij.** $10.00-15.00
- ❑ **GI9719 Blonde Comme Les.** $10.00-15.00
- ❑ **GI9720 Et Si On.** $10.00-15.00
- ❑ **GI9721 Heb Ji Geen Dorst?** $10.00-15.00
- ❑ **GI9722 Zwelen We Samen.** $10.00-15.00
- ❑ **GI9723 T'as Pas Soif Toi?** $10.00-15.00

Comments: Belgium sold sixteen different beer glasses. They consisted of two different beer distributors, four different designs, and two different languages printed on the glasses. Each glass represented one beer company, one design, one language, yielding a total of sixteen different glasses.

GI9716-17

Stella Artois counter card.

GI9718-19

Center: GI9720-23

Bottom: GI9720-23 reverse side.

1998

• 14th National Owners Operators Convention

Place: Orlando, Florida
Date: March 16-19, 1998
Theme: "The Value of Gold"

Cardinals Legendary Players Glasses, 1998

❑ **GI9802 Ozzie Smith.** $8.00-10.00
❑ **GI9803 Lou Brock.** $8.00-10.00
❑ **GI9804 Mark McGwire.** $15.00-20.00
❑ **GI9805 Bob Gibson.** $8.00-10.00

Comments: Set of four clear glasses featured the players and their statistics. Set was only distributed in the St. Louis, Missouri regional area.

GI9802-05

GI9802-05

Orioles Greatest Moment Glasses, 1998

- ❑ **GI9806 Immortal Cal.** $3.00-5.00
- ❑ **GI9807 Four Straight.** $3.00-5.00
- ❑ **GI9808 Defeat Chicago.** $3.00-5.00
- ❑ **GI9809 World Champions.** $3.00-5.00
- ❑ **GI9810 Memorial Stadium.** $3.00-5.00
- ❑ **GI9811 Orioles Soar.** $3.00-5.00

Comments: Orioles set of six clear glasses were distributed in the Baltimore / Washington D.C. area only. Each heavy glass has *The Baltimore Sun* newspaper headlines representing an accomplishment.

GI9806-08

GI9809-11

NASCAR Glasses, 1998

- ❏ **GI9812 Red NASCAR with McDonald's and Coke logos.** $4.00-5.00
- ❏ **GI9813 Blue NASCAR.** $4.00-5.00
- ❏ **GI9814 Red NASCAR with Ronald's face.** $4.00-5.00
- ❏ **GI9815 Yellow NASCAR.** $4.00-5.00

Comments: NASCAR set of four glasses were sold in areas near the NASCAR Racing Tracks.

GI9812-15

NASCAR glasses translite.

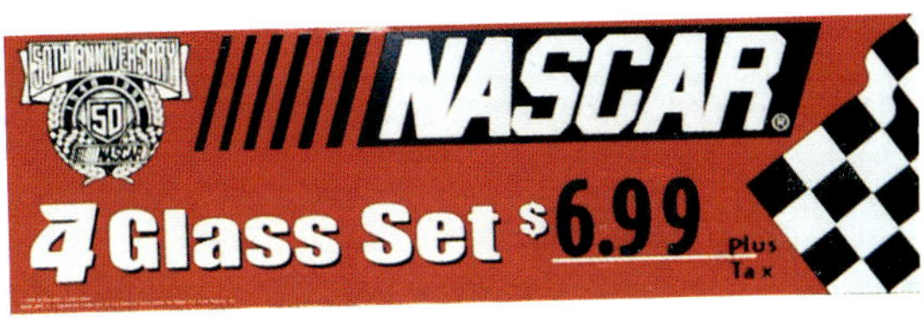

International Animal Kingdom Glasses, 1998

- ❑ **GL9820 Animal Kingdom - Goofy, pedestal style.** $8.00-10.00
- ❑ **GL9821 Animal Kingdom - Mickey Mouse, pedestal style.** $8.00-10.00
- ❑ **GL9822 Animal Kingdom - Minnie Mouse, indented base.** $8.00-10.00
- ❑ **GL9823 Animal Kingdom - Donald Duck, pedestal style.** $8.00-10.00

Comments: Celebrates the opening of the Animal Kingdom Wildlife Park in Walt Disney World, Orlando, Florida. The set of four Animal Kingdom glasses was sold over the counter at McDonald's restaurants in Japan. Each glass came packaged in a separate box. The Walt Disney World Resorts logo is on one side of the glass and the McDonald's logo on the other side.

GI9820-23

Generic Glasses and Mugs, 1998

❑ **GI9801 Chevron & McDonald's Wine Glass.** Chevron and McDonald's teamed up with an introductory glass given out at Chevron-McDonald's openings. $10.00-20.00

GI9801

GI9801

❑ **GI9816 Monopoly PLAY THE GAME Mug.** Cream colored mug featured Monopoly graphics in red, white, black, and gold. $2.00-3.00

❑ **GI9817 International France Electricity Monopoly Glass.** Clear glass with the Electricity Utilities light bulb featured. First in a series of two. $15.00-25.00

GI9816

GI9817-18

❑ **GI9818 International France Water Monopoly Glass.** Clear glass with Water Utilities featured. Second in a series of two.
$15.00-25.00

❑ **GI9819 International Japan Nagano Glass.** Glass has a picture of a green lilac and yellow Snowlet skiing. The Nagano logo and the McDonald's logo are both imprinted in blue on the back. Came in a box with Japanese and English writing.
$25.00-35.00

GI9817 (front)

GI9817(back)

Index